Better Homes and Gardens®

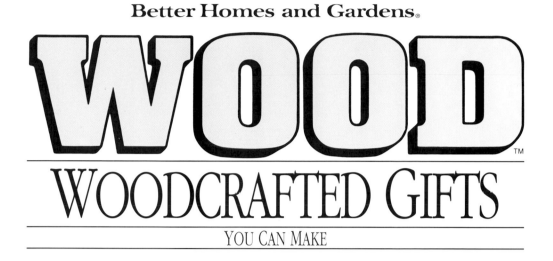

WOOD™
WOODCRAFTED GIFTS
YOU CAN MAKE

All of us at Meredith® Books are dedicated to giving you the
information and ideas you need to create beautiful and useful
woodworking projects. We guarantee your satisfaction with this
book for as long as you own it. We also welcome your comments
and suggestions. Please write us at Meredith® Books, BB-117,
1100 Walnut St., Des Moines, IA 50309-3400.

A **WOOD**™ **BOOK**
Published by Meredith® Books

MEREDITH® BOOKS
President, Book Group: Joseph J. Ward
Vice President and Editorial Director: Elizabeth P. Rice
Executive Editor: Connie Schrader
Art Director: Ernest Shelton
Prepress Production Manager: Randall Yontz

WOOD® MAGAZINE
President, Magazine Group: William T. Kerr
Editor: Larry Clayton

WOODCRAFTED GIFTS YOU CAN MAKE
Produced by Roundtable Press, Inc.
Directors: Susan E. Meyer, Marsha Melnick
Senior Editors: Sue Heinemann, Virginia Croft
Managing Editor: Ross L. Horowitz
Graphic Designer: Jeff Fitschen
Design Assistant: Leslie Goldman
Art Assistant: Ahmad Mallah
Copy Assistant: Amy Handy

For Meredith® Books
Editorial Project Manager/Assistant Art Director: Tom Wegner
Contributing How-To Editors: Marlen Kemmet,
    Charles E. Sommers
Contributing Techniques Editor: Bill Krier
Contributing Tool Editor: Larry Johnston
Contributing Outline Editor: David A. Kirchner

Special thanks to Khristy Benoit

On the front cover: Acorn Treasure Box, pages 9–11

On the back cover (clockwise from top left): Quilt-Look
    Hand Mirror, pages 59–60, Quality-Crafted Pendulum
    Cradle, pages 69-73, Fortune-Four Desk Accessories,
    pages 44-49

Meredith Corporation Corporate Officers:
Chairman of the Executive Committee: E. T. Meredith III
Chairman of the Board, President and Chief Executive Officer:
    Jack D. Rehm
Group Presidents: Joseph J. Ward, Books; William T. Kerr, Magazines;
    Philip A. Jones, Broadcasting; Allen L. Sabbag, Real Estate
Vice Presidents: Leo R. Armatis, Corporate Relations;
    Thomas G. Fisher, General Counsel and Secretary;
    Larry D. Hartsook, Finance; Michael A. Sell, Treasurer;
    Kathleen J. Zehr, Controller and Assistant Secretary

FOR DISPLAY AND DECORATION 4
BAND-SAWN SCALLOP BOXES 5
WEED POTS SCRAPWOOD SPECIAL 8
ACORN TREASURE BOX 9
WILY-FOX WEATHER VANE 12
GARDENING WITH A GOUGE 14
HANGING-GARDEN PLANTER BASKET 18
HEIRLOOM QUILT HANGER 20
BOOK OF MEMORIES 24

FROM THE DESK OF... 28
LAMINATED LETTER OPENER 29
THE MINI-SAFE AND BILL BOX OR KEY KEEPER 31
EXECUTIVE PAPERWEIGHT 34
TAKING CARE OF BUSINESS CARD CASE 36
READY-REFERENCE CALENDAR/CLOCK 38
NEW HORIZON DESK SET 40
FORTUNE-FOUR DESK ACCESSORIES 44
EXECUTIVE NAMEPLATE 50
WHALE STAMP BOX 52
WRITE STUFF HARDWOOD PENS 54
NOTEWORTHY NOTEPAD HOLDERS 56

HER FAVORITE THINGS 58
QUILT-LOOK HAND MIRROR 59
PERFUME DECANTER 61
"JUST FOR HER" NECKLACE 63
COUNTRY-STYLE SWAN NECKLACE 64
AUTUMN DELIGHT WOODEN NECKLACE 65
SWEETHEART STICKPIN 66
DESIGNER EARRINGS 67
BRING ON THE BRACELETS 68
QUALITY-CRAFTED PENDULUM CRADLE 69

FOR THE KITCHEN WITH LOVE 74
ROLLING-PIN RECIPE-CARD HOLDER 75
MAKE 'EM IN A DASH SHAKERS 76
SPICED-UP NAPKIN HOLDER 78
NO-PROBLEM PIZZA PADDLE 80
GET A HANDLE ON THESE SHARP STEAK KNIVES 82
WELL-ORDERED CUTLERY CASE 84
STRAIGHT 'N' NARROW NOODLE CUTTER 86
WALNUT-CLAD PUMP DISPENSER 88
SUNBURST SINK BOARD 90
HOT-STUFF OAK SERVER 94

FOR DISPLAY AND DECORATION

Create charming gifts for the home with any of the projects that follow. As an added bonus, some are small enough to be made from the scraps you have saved from other wood projects.

BAND-SAWN SCALLOP BOXES

When we saw our first band-sawn boxes at a crafts fair a few years ago, we were amazed. How could a single piece of wood and a bandsaw yield projects of such beauty? Actually, as we found out, they're much easier to make than you might imagine. With our tidal wave of accompanying photos, you'll have no difficulty crafting the scallop boxes shown *opposite* on your band-saw. These little treasure chests work great for housing anything from a string of pearls at home to paper clips at the office.

Cutting and shaping the box parts

1. Start by cutting a block of wood to 2¼" high by 4" wide by 6" long, or laminate thinner stock to size. Sand the top and bottom of the block smooth. (The stock for two of our boxes came from the firewood pile.)

2. Using carbon paper or a photocopy machine, transfer the full-size Top View pattern on *page 7* to a piece of paper. Cut the paper pattern to shape, making sure you don't cut away any of the exterior pattern lines. Apply spray adhesive to the back of the pattern; then adhere it to the top of the wood block.

3. Fit your bandsaw with a ⅛" blade. (This fine-toothed blade makes cutting the curves a snap.) Make a series of relief cuts where shown in photo A *below left*. Then, cut the box exterior to shape, cutting just outside the marked line. Sand the sawn sides smooth.

4. Position the fence on your bandsaw ⁵⁄₁₆" away from the *inside* edge of the blade. Now, *slowly and carefully* slice ⁵⁄₁₆" off the top face of the block for the *lid* and ⁵⁄₁₆" off the bottom face for the *base* as shown in photo B *below left*.

5. Cut the lid to finished shape as shown in photo C on *page 6*. Sand the two edges you just cut.

6. Set the box lid aside for now. Then, using the full-size Body pattern on *page 7* as reference, *continued*

A

Cut slightly outside the marked perimeter line to cut box to shape.

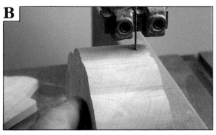

B

With the fence for support, cut the lid and then the base from the box.

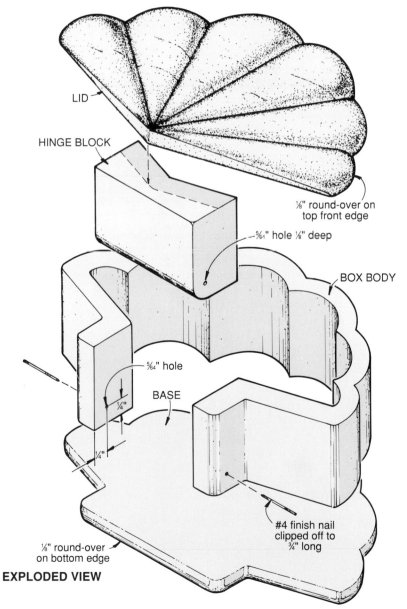

LID

HINGE BLOCK

⅛" round-over on top front edge

⁵⁄₆₄" hole ⅛" deep

BOX BODY

⁵⁄₆₄" hole

BASE

¼"

¼"

#4 finish nail clipped off to ¾" long

⅛" round-over on bottom edge

EXPLODED VIEW

BAND-SAWN SCALLOP BOXES
continued

transfer the straight and scalloped lines to the box body as shown in photo D.

7. Carefully cut along the *inside* edge of the line just drawn on the box body, following the route shown in photo E. *Save* the small wedge-shaped cutout; you'll use it later for the lid hinge.

8. To sand the interior curved areas of the box body, wrap 100-grit sandpaper around lengths of ⅜"- and ¾"-diameter dowels (see photo F). Sand the other interior surfaces smooth too.

9. Sand the top face of the base smooth. (To keep the base flat while sanding, we taped a full sheet of 100-, and later 150-grit, sandpaper to a flat surface and moved the base back and forth evenly on the sandpaper.)

10. To glue the base onto the box body, start by clamping the hinge block (no glue) back into its original position as shown in photo G (the hinge block serves only as a spacer at this point). To prevent the hinge block from being too tight when installed later, place thick paper or thin cardboard spacers between the hinge block ends and the box body where shown in the photo. Cover the bottom face of the hinge block with tape to prevent it from being glued to the base. Finally, glue the base to the box body. After the glue dries, remove the clamps and the hinge block. Sand the edges of the base flush with the outside edges of the box body.

"Sculpting" the box lid

1. Using double-faced tape, tape the lid (pattern side up) to the corner of the workbench top. Then, cut kerfs through the paper pattern and into the lid as shown in photo H. (We used a dovetail saw; a backsaw also will work.) The kerfs should be ⅛" deep at the front of the lid and barely scratch the surface at the hinge end. (We used a combination square to mark the ⅛" kerf depths on the front edge of the lid.)

2. With a sharp 1¼" chisel, make paring cuts starting at the marked

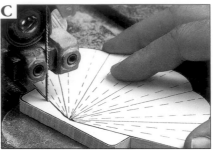

Follow the marked lines to cut the lid to finished shape on the bandsaw.

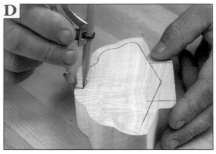

Use a compass and sharp pencil to mark the box's curved interior lines.

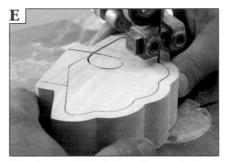

Slowly, carefully follow the marked lines to cut the box's interior to shape.

Wrap sandpaper around a dowel to sand the interior curves smooth.

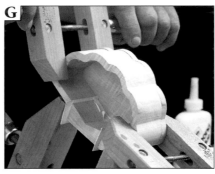

Handscrews make clamping the base back onto the box body easy.

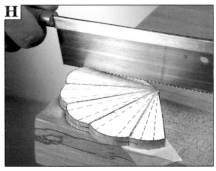

Cut angled kerfs with a fine-toothed saw at the marked lines.

chisel lines and ending at the kerf as shown in photo I.

3. Sand the chiseled surfaces smooth, forming a round-over like that shown in the photograph on *page 4*.

Final assembly and fitting

1. Sand a ¼" round-over on the bottom back edge of the hinge block where shown on the Hinge Block Side View drawing, *opposite*. Then, sand the hinge block smooth.

2. Position the hinge block in the box body, centering it from side to side and flush with the top and

Sculpt the lid top to rough shape with a sharp 1¼" chisel.

back edges (we used paper spacers to center and hold it in position). Drill a ⁵⁄₆₄" hole on each side of the box body ⁵⁄₈" deep into the hinge block where shown on Exploded View drawing on *page 5,* and temporarily insert the #4 finish nails.

3. Position the lid on the box body with its back edges flush with those of the box. Mark the lid location outline on top of the hinge block. Remove the lid and hinge block from the box body. Glue and clamp the lid to the hinge where marked.

4. Position the lid assembly back onto the box body, and again temporarily insert the hinge nails. Sand the front edge of the lid flush with that of the box body. Sand a ⅛" round-over along the bottom outside edge of the base and top outside edge of the lid where shown on the Exploded View drawing. Sand the base and lid. (We sanded with progressively finer [100- to 320-grit] sandpaper.) Remove the lid assembly from the box body.

5. Apply the finish to the box body and lid assembly (we sprayed on three coats of lacquer). Rub the surface with #0000 steel wool between coats. After the final coat of lacquer has dried, rub the surface with steel wool loaded with finishing wax.

6. Snip the heads off the two hinge nails. Position the lid on the base, insert the hinge nails, and set both nails. Fill the nail holes with a putty that matches the wood's color.

Project Tool List
Tablesaw
Bandsaw
Portable drill
 ⁵⁄₆₄" bit
Finishing sander

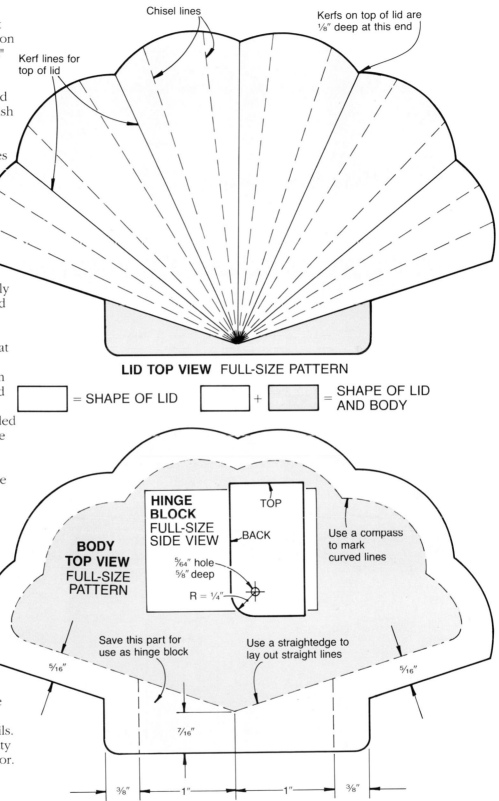

Chisel lines

Kerf lines for top of lid

Kerfs on top of lid are ⅛" deep at this end

LID TOP VIEW FULL-SIZE PATTERN

☐ = SHAPE OF LID   ☐ + ▨ = SHAPE OF LID AND BODY

HINGE BLOCK FULL-SIZE SIDE VIEW

TOP

BACK

⁵⁄₆₄" hole ⁵⁄₈" deep

R = ¼"

BODY TOP VIEW FULL-SIZE PATTERN

Use a compass to mark curved lines

Save this part for use as hinge block

Use a straightedge to lay out straight lines

⁵⁄₁₆"   ⁵⁄₁₆"

⁷⁄₁₆"

⅜"   1"   1"   ⅜"

Note: We built the project using the tools listed. You may be able to substitute other tools or equipment for listed items you don't have.

Additional common hand tools and clamps may be required to complete the project.

WEED POTS SCRAPWOOD SPECIAL

It never fails! You cut a board to length and end up with a tail-end piece that's just a hair too short for anything but the scrap box. Here's an excellent idea using those shop leftovers: decorative weed pots.

1. For the laminated pot shown in the photo at *left*, cut one piece of ½" oak and two pieces of ¾" walnut scrapwood to roughly 7" square. Laminate the oak between the walnut, sandwich fashion, keeping the bottom edges as flush as possible. For the solid-oak weed pot, use a single piece of 1½"-thick scrap or laminate two ¾" pieces. (Feel free to experiment with other woods.)

2. Using a compass, mark a 6"-diameter circle, leaving a flat bottom approximately 2½" long, where shown in the Front View drawing *below*.

3. Use a bandsaw or jigsaw to cut the pot to shape. Remove the saw marks from the edges of the pot by rotating it on a belt sander clamped to your workbench top. Hold the pot perpendicular while you sand the edges, especially when sanding the bottom, so that the pot will rest square later.

4. Locate the center of the base on one side of the pot. Then, use a square to mark the corresponding point on the top of the pot for the stem hole you will drill later.

5. Use a router with a ⅜" round-over bit to rout the edges.

6. With a 1" flat-bottomed bit, bore a 3½"-deep stem hole into the top of the pot. (If you want to use the pot for fresh-cut flowers, waterproof the hole with epoxy: Pour an ounce or two of epoxy into the hole and rotate the pot to spread an even coat inside the hole.)

7. Finish-sand the outside of the pot with progressively finer sandpaper, starting with 100 grit and finishing with 220 grit. The exposed end grain will require additional sanding.

8. Finish the weed pot with tung oil or polyurethane, including the stem hole (if you didn't coat it with epoxy earlier).

Project Tool List
Tablesaw
Bandsaw or portable jigsaw
Belt sander
Drill press or portable drill
  1" bit
Router
  ⅜" round-over bit
Finishing sander

Note: *We built the project using the tools listed. You may be able to substitute other tools or equipment for listed items you don't have. Additional common hand tools and clamps may be required to complete the project.*

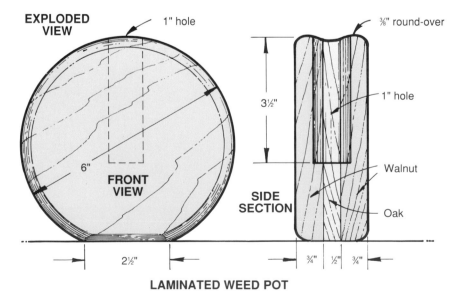

EXPLODED VIEW

1" hole

⅜" round-over

6"

FRONT VIEW

3½"

1" hole

SIDE SECTION

Walnut

Oak

2½"

¾" ½" ¾"

LAMINATED WEED POT

ACORN TREASURE BOX

Not all acorns grow on trees. This clever turning project developed on our lathe in only two hours, and that's taking time out for coffee. We began with a 3×3×6" mahogany turning square, turned it to a cylinder, and then shaped the cap and hollow nut. What a way to gift wrap jewelry for a loved one!

Prepare the turning stock

1. To make this acorn, start with a 3×3×6" turning blank. (We used Honduras mahogany. See the Buying Guide on *page 11* for our source.) Locate the centerpoint of each end of the blank by drawing diagonals. Center a 3" faceplate on one end, mark the hole centerpoints, and drill the pilot holes. Then, fasten the faceplate to

the blank with #10×1" sheet-metal screws. (We've found that sheet-metal screws grip the stock tighter than wood screws.)

2. Next, secure the faceplate onto the lathe headstock spindle. Slide the tailstock up to the center-point of the free end, and lock it. Now, with the stock firmly mounted between centers, start the lathe, and turn the blank to a 2⅞"-diameter cylinder. (We used a 1" gouge and our lathe's slowest speed [600 rpm].)

3. Using the dimensions on drawing A *below left*, pencil lines on the cylinder to help locate the cap and nut as shown on drawing B. When finished, back the tailstock away from the square.

4. Make cardboard templates for the cap and nut from the full-sized Section View drawing on *page 10*.

Turn the cap first

1. Increase your lathe speed (we shaped the cap and nut at 800 to 1,000 rpms). Using a ¼" parting tool, start cutting the recess in the cap using the dimensions shown on the Cap Profile drawing *below*. Next, switch to a ⅜" gouge and hollow the cap's interior. Then, as shown on drawing C on *page 10*, turn a slight taper on the inside rim *continued*

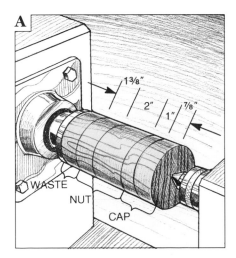

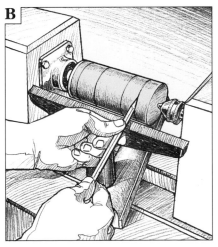

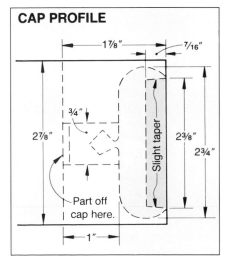

CAP PROFILE

ACORN TREASURE BOX
continued

SECTION VIEW

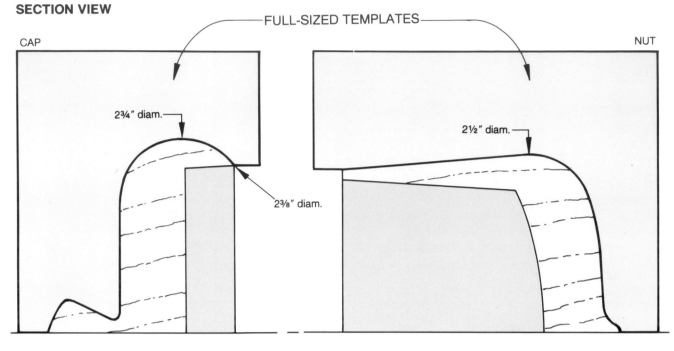

FULL-SIZED TEMPLATES

CAP

NUT

2¾″ diam.

2⅜″ diam.

2½″ diam.

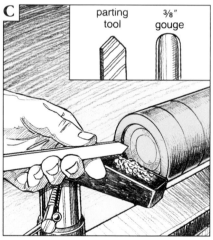

C

parting tool   ⅜″ gouge

the cap. Then, using a parting tool, separate the cap from the turning stock as shown on drawing D *below*.

Turn the nut to shape and finish the cap

1. Reduce the lathe's speed to 1,000 rpm and square the face of the remaining turning stock.

2. Next, with a ⅜″ gouge, turn a taper on the cylinder toward the free end. It should be slightly larger in diameter than the inside of the cap. Now, sand the taper until the cap fits snugly onto it. Twist the cap onto the end of the taper.

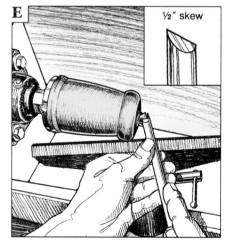

E

½″ skew

of the cap with the parting tool. This taper will allow the cap to fit snugly onto the nut. Finally, sand the recess smooth with 100-, 150-, and 220-grit sandpaper.

2. Next, shape the outside of the cap using a ⅜″ gouge and the cap template you made earlier as a guide. Turn the stem area between the cap and nut stock to ¾″ diameter.

3. Increase your lathe speed (we run ours at 1,200 to 1,500 rpm for most sanding), and sand the top of

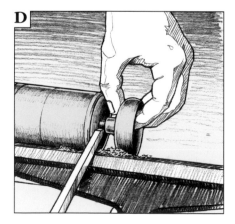

D

Finish turning the cap's stem to shape (we used a ½″ skew) as shown on drawing E *above.*

3. Finish-sand the top of the cap and the stem. Then, remove the cap from the tapered cylinder.

4. Using a ⅜″ gouge and the nut templates as a guide, remove some of the excess stock (about an inch) from the waste area at the base of the acorn. (We found that removing this stock gave us a better idea of how deep to turn the inside of the nut.)

5. Hollow out the inside of the nut as shown on drawing F. (We used a ½" gouge, but a round-nosed scraper would work equally well). Turn the wall to just over ⅛" thick at the opening, and the nut bottom to ¼" thick. Now sand the interior smooth.

6. Using the dimensions on the Nut Profile drawing at *right,* and the nut template as guides, finish turning the bottom of the acorn to shape. (We used our ⅜" gouge for this.) Leave a ½" dowel-like connection between the waste and nut bottom. Sand the exterior of the nut smooth.

7. Next, using a parting tool, turn a small nub on the center of the nut bottom. The nub allows the acorn to rest at a slight angle, adding realism to the final look. (When turning the bottom, we

NUT PROFILE

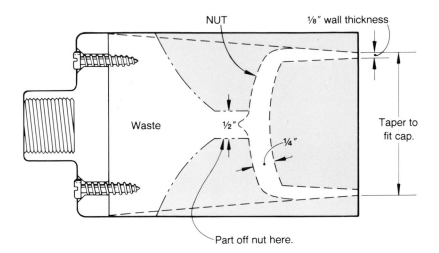

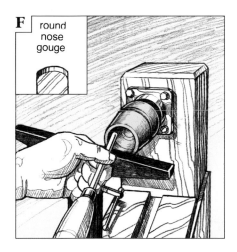

F   round nose gouge

turned away a little material at a time, then sanded with the lathe running. We turned closer to the center and sanded some more. This helped prepare the surface of the nut for finishing.)

8. Now, part the nut from the waste. Catch the nut with your hand; don't let it spin off and hit the floor.

Now, finish the acorn

1. Hand-sand the nut if necessary. (Ours required a bit of sanding around the nub.)

2. Stain and finish the acorn. (We stained the cap a walnut color, and the nut a light maple). Let the stain dry overnight, then apply the finish. (We spray-applied three coats of lacquer, sanding between coats.)

Buying Guide
• **Turning square.** Honduras mahogany, 3x3x12". For current prices, contact Constantine, 2050 Eastchester Rd., Bronx, NY 10461, or call 800-223-8087.

Project Tool List
Lathe
    3" faceplate
    Tail center
    ⅜", ½" gouges
    ⅛" parting tool
    ½" skew

Note: We built the project using the tools listed. You may be able to substitute other tools or equipment for listed items you don't have. Additional common hand tools and clamps may be required to complete the project.

WILY-FOX WEATHER VANE

This quick red(wood) fox is more than a pretty cutout. Scroll- or bandsaw it with our pattern, then complete the simple weather-vane plan, and turn the fox out to keep watch on the wind.

1. Enlarge the Fox pattern, *opposite,* with an enlarging copier or gridded paper, and transfer it to a ¾X8X24" piece of redwood. Align the feet of the fox with one edge of the board. (We applied a photo-copy enlargement to the wood with spray adhesive, but a carbon-paper tracing also works.)

2. Cut the outline with a scroll-saw (we used a #11 skip-tooth blade), and then drill a ³⁄₃₂" start hole where indicated on the

pattern. Thread the blade through the hole to make the interior cut between the tail and hind leg. If you are cutting the fox with a bandsaw, notice the optional entry cut marked on the pattern.

3. Mark the location for the pivot-tube hole on the bottom edge of the fox, where shown on the pattern. The hole must be straight and vertical, so we used a doweling jig as a drill guide. Install the jig loosely, put a dowel into the drill hole, and adjust the jig so that the dowel is aligned with the reference line on the plan. Then, tighten the jig, remove the dowel, and drill the hole 3¾" deep with a ⁵⁄₁₆" brad-point bit.

4. Next, select a piece of 1½X1½" stock (we used redwood) of

appropriate length for your mounting post. Center and drill a ¼" hole 2" deep and then cut ½" chamfers at one end.

5. Hacksaw ½" from one end of a brass toilet-tank float rod, available from a home center or hardware store. Coat the short piece with epoxy and insert it into one end of a 3¾"-long piece of ¼" copper tube. Now, cut the float rod to 10" overall, leaving the long threads on the uncut end. With a grinder or disc sander, grind the cut end to a point. (See the Post detail *opposite.*)

6. Coat the threaded end of the float rod with epoxy and then insert it into the hole at the top of the mounting post.

7. Sand the outside of the copper tube with 60-grit sandpaper, coat it

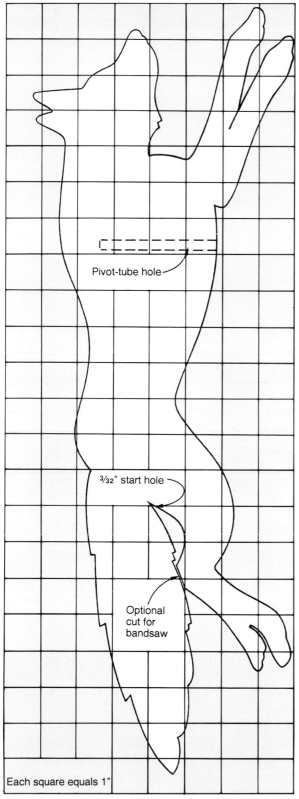

Pivot-tube hole

³⁄₃₂" start hole

Optional
cut for
bandsaw

Each square equals 1"

To enlarge this pattern on a photocopying machine, set the copier's enlargement ratio at 141 percent. Copy the pattern, then enlarge the copy at 141 percent. Enlarge the resulting copy again; this time in sections at 121 percent. Join the pieces with cellophane tape for a full pattern.

with epoxy, and press it into the hole in the fox. Insert the closed end first. Drill into the brass piece inside the tube with a ¼" twist bit to form a cone.

8. Sand the fox and post, and round over the edges slightly with sandpaper. Coat the fox and mounting post with a clear, penetrating, waterproofing finish (we used Olympic Wood Preservative) before putting him to work out in the yard.

Project Tool List
Tablesaw
Scrollsaw or bandsaw
Portable drill
    Doweling jig
    Bits: ³⁄₃₂", ¼", ⁵⁄₁₆"
Disc sander
Finishing sander

Note: *We built the project using the tools listed. You may be able to substitute other tools or equipment for listed items you don't have. Additional common hand tools and clamps may be required to complete the project.*

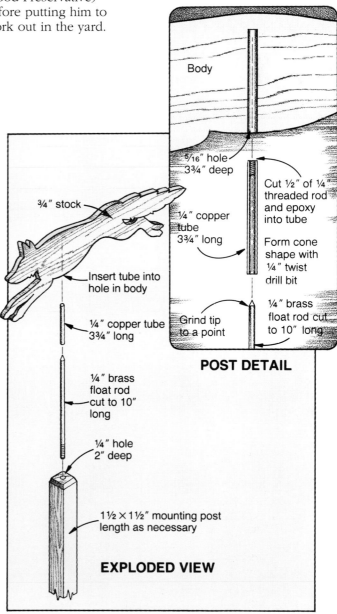

Body

⁵⁄₁₆" hole
3¾" deep

Cut ½" of ¼" threaded rod and epoxy into tube

Form cone shape with ¼" twist drill bit

¼" brass float rod cut to 10" long

¾" stock

¼" copper tube 3¾" long

Insert tube into hole in body

Grind tip to a point

POST DETAIL

¼" copper tube 3¾" long

¼" brass float rod cut to 10" long

¼" hole 2" deep

1½ × 1½" mounting post length as necessary

EXPLODED VIEW

GARDENING WITH A GOUGE

Bring springtime into any room with this ever-blooming daffodil. It calls for some carving skill but is easy to make.

1. Locate the center on top of a 2x4x4" block. Trace the full-sized flower pattern, *opposite,* onto it, centering the pattern over the block center.

2. Adjust the pilot bit of a 2" holesaw (inside diameter approximately 1¾") so it projects ¼" or less beyond the cutting edge. With the holesaw chucked into your drill press, pilot on the center mark to bore 1" deep, forming a cylinder that will become the flower's trumpet. Change to a ½" bit, and drill 1" deep, following the pilot hole. (We held the block with a handscrew clamp.)

3. Mark the center on the bottom of the piece, and bore ½" deep with a 1" holesaw (inside diameter about ¾"). Again, set the pilot bit for minimum protrusion. Then, cut around the pattern outline with a bandsaw or scrollsaw.

Rough out the flower

1. Divide the flower blank into four equal horizontal segments by drawing three parallel lines ½" apart around the sides. Place the first line ½" from the top, as shown on the Flower Cross Section drawing, *opposite.*

2. Next, brace the blank against a bench stop, and remove the top ½" section of the petals with a 10mm or larger no. 5 or no. 7 gouge. (You could make quick work of this by using a ¾" carpenter's chisel,

too.) Do not cut away any of the central cylinder—leave it full height. Grain direction changes from petal to petal, so be careful to avoid chip-out.

3. Draw the curved petal top line between the point of each petal on the upper line and the base at the next lower line, as shown on the Flower Cross Section drawing. Accurate curves aren't critical here; you can draw the lines freehand. Carve down to them with your gouge as shown *below left.*

Fashion the flower's trumpet

1. Next, rough out the trumpet. Mark off the flared lip with two pencil lines, one around the side of the cylinder ¼" from the top and a circle on the top ³⁄₁₆" in from the side. Stop-cut the line you drew around the side. Also stop-cut the base of the cylinder where it meets the petals. (A *stop cut,* an incision along a pattern line, allows you to carve up to a line without chipping out wood beyond it.) Form a funnel shape between the lip and the petal surface, as shown *below.* The no. 7 or no. 9 gouge and your knife will come in handy as you carve a smooth curve to a bottom diameter of about 1". Be careful not

As you carve down to the petal top line, take care to avoid chip-out near the petal tips and bases.

Form the trumpet shape by carving down from beneath the trumpet lip to petal surface.

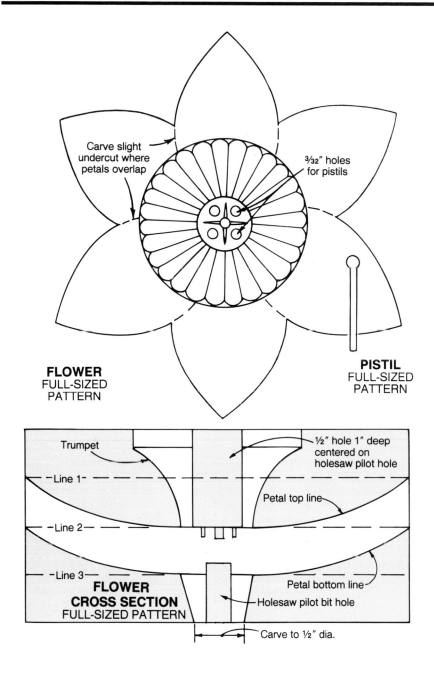

Carve slight undercut where petals overlap

³⁄₃₂" holes for pistils

FLOWER
FULL-SIZED
PATTERN

PISTIL
FULL-SIZED
PATTERN

Trumpet

½" hole 1" deep centered on holesaw pilot hole

— Line 1 —

Petal top line

— Line 2 —

— Line 3 —

FLOWER CROSS SECTION
FULL-SIZED PATTERN

Petal bottom line

Holesaw pilot bit hole

Carve to ½" dia.

3. Begin carving the petals by shaping their bottoms. Undercut the edges of the overlapping petals to accentuate the separation as shown at *right*. Carve each petal to a spoon shape on top, matching the bottom curve. Undercut the overlapping top edges. Make the petals about ⅛" thick at the center, tapering to about ¹⁄₁₆" at the edge for a delicate look. Sand smooth on both sides.

Take time to refine the trumpet

1. Since it will be the carving's most prominent feature, take extra care in detailing the trumpet. Reduce the wall thickness to about ⅛" as you refine the shape and smooth the surface. Draw pencil lines vertically on the inside and outside of the trumpet, dividing it into four sections. Subdivide each of those roughly into thirds. Don't try to make all 12 sections exactly equal—that wouldn't look natural.

2. With a small V-tool, carve along the guidelines inside and outside to give the impression of creases. Bring the carving line over the edge of the trumpet rim, and then widen the notch with your knife to create a scalloped effect. Carve V-tool grooves about ⅝" long on the top of the lip between the lines to heighten the scalloped look. Sand the trumpet, softening

continued

Carve alternate petals to full shape, and undercut the edges to create the illusion of separate, overlapping petals.

to snap the trumpet off—the ½" hole leaves a thin wall at the bottom.

2. Rough out the inside of the trumpet with your knife and gouges, matching the inside contour to the outside shape. (You could shape the trumpet with a flexible shaft machine or hand-held rotary tool and cutting burrs, too.)

Create natural-looking petals

1. Draw the petal bottom lines parallel to the top lines and ½"

below them. Cut away the bottom ½" section of the petals, and then carve to the petal bottom lines. Taper the calyx (the cylinder on the bottom of the flower) to about ½" diameter at the end.

2. The petals overlap each other alternately. Indicate the petals, which will be entirely visible from the top by drawing pencil guidelines (shown on the full-sized pattern), and then draw similar lines on the *opposite* petals on the bottom.

GARDENING WITH A GOUGE
continued

any sharp edges. A conical rotary burr works well to detail the trumpet, too, as shown *below*.

3. Carve five pistils about ³⁄₃₂" diameter with a ball on one end from ³⁄₁₆" square stock 1¼" long. Drill ³⁄₃₂" holes where shown on the pattern, and then glue the pistils into the holes with the tops about ¹⁄₁₆" below the trumpet rim.

Now, make the stem

1. Trace the full-sized pattern for the upper stem onto a ½x2x14" piece of basswood. Extend the lower part, making the stem 14" long overall. Bandsaw the stem blank, and then drill a hole the size of the one in the flower where shown.

2. Carve the top to ½" diameter as far back as the dotted line on the pattern. Then, study the flower photo on *page 14,* noticing how the green stem emerges from the brown bud shield.

3. Round the edge just below the upper stem, and then carve the long, oval bud-shield opening. The

A handheld rotary tool with a conical carbide or ruby burr does a great job on trumpet details. You could carve the entire flower with power tools.

top of the shield forms a rounded point. Hollow it out about ³⁄₁₆" deep above the stem. Form a slight bead where shown. Carve the stem below it to about ¼" diameter.

A lesson in leaves

1. Carve the leaves from five pieces of ¾x¾" basswood, four 10" long and one 8" long. On each, mark off a 3" section approximately in the middle for the transition area where you will carve around a corner to create a cupped, twisted leaf.

2. Draw two parallel lines about ½" apart along one side of the stock from the bottom to the transition zone. There, curve the lines to the edge and continue them on the adjacent face—either left or right. Bring them to a gentle point at the top, shown in the Leaf Layout drawing at *right.*

3. Gouge out a groove about ³⁄₁₆" deep between the lines. Then, rough out the back of the leaf with your knife. Make the finished leaf about ³⁄₁₆" thick at the center, with thin edges.

Paint it, and pot it

1. Attach the flower to the stem with a ¼" dowel (or one to fit the pilot hole). Fair the stem and calyx. Sand, and then paint all parts except the bud shield on the stem with gesso, a white primer. Sand the gesso coat smooth. Mask off the stem and flower, and then coat the bud shield with clear spray lacquer. Paint the flower with yellow acrylic paint. (See the supplies list for the colors we used.) Bring the green of the leaves and stem up onto the calyx, almost to the petals.

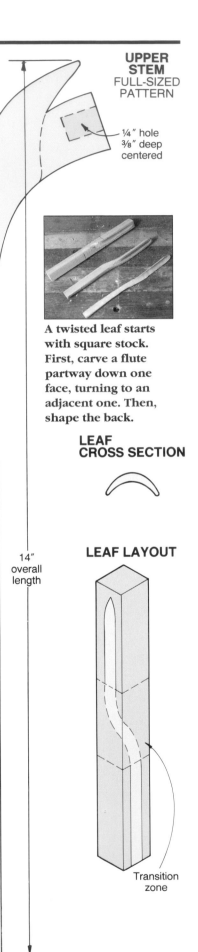

UPPER STEM
FULL-SIZED PATTERN

¼" hole
³⁄₈" deep
centered

A twisted leaf starts with square stock. First, carve a flute partway down one face, turning to an adjacent one. Then, shape the back.

LEAF CROSS SECTION

LEAF LAYOUT

14" overall length

Transition zone

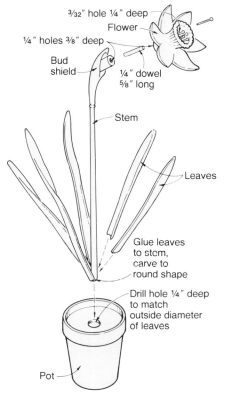

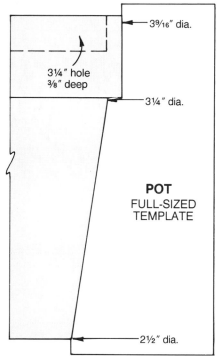

POT
FULL-SIZED
TEMPLATE

3⁹/₁₆" dia.

3¼" hole
3/8" deep

3¼" dia.

2½" dia.

SUPPLIES

Stock

Basswood 2x4x4" for flower, ½x2x14" for stem, four ¾x¾x10" and one ¾x¾x8" for leaves, 4x4x6" for pot.

Gouges

10mm or larger no. 7, no. 5 5mm no. 9

V-Tools

6mm no. 12, 4mm no. 12

Knife

Bench knife

Power carver (optional)

Rotary carver with burrs

Finishing

Aerosol clear lacquer
Liquitex acrylic paints
•Gesso—primer
•Cadmium yellow medium
•Chromium oxide green
•Burnt umber
•Brilliant orange

Project Tool List

Tablesaw
Scrollsaw or bandsaw
Drill press
Portable drill
    Holesaws: 2", 1"
    Bits: ³/₃₂", ¼", ½"
Lathe and turning tools

Note: *We built the project using the tools listed. You may be able to substitute other tools or equipment for listed items you don't have. Additional common hand tools and clamps may be required to complete the project.*

2. File, sand, or carve the bottoms of the four long leaves to fit together around the stem. Glue them to the stem, clamping with a heavy rubber band. Place a small spacer block between each leaf and the stem until the glue dries. Insert the short leaf between the stem and any other leaf.

3. Carve the bottom to a drill-bit diameter. Turn a flowerpot using the template, *above right,* and drill a hole for the stem. Paint the soil burnt umber and the pot orange mixed with burnt umber.

HANGING-GARDEN PLANTER BASKET

Like a gentle hand, this contemporary redwood planter supports your favorite potted plant, letting it drink in sunlight while its leaves cascade down. It accepts pots with up to a 5¼"-diameter base. Metal rings attached to the support arm allow the planter to swing in the wind and hang from an overhead fastener. Our template makes the construction a breeze.

First, cut the basket pieces and make the jig

1. Rip 25' of ¾X¾" strips from a ¾"X5½"X72" redwood board. (See the Cutting Diagram at *right*).

2. From the strips, crosscut 49 pieces (A) to 5½". (We used a power miter saw and a stopblock to saw duplicate pieces.) Cut the support arm (B) to ¾X¾X16½".

3. Using the Planter Assembly drawing *opposite, top,* for hole locations, drill ⅜" holes through both ends of the arm, and through one end of one part A. Cut three ¾"-long lengths of ⅜" rigid copper tubing and drive one into each of these holes for the rigid bushings.

4. From ¾"-thick particleboard (we started with a 24X48" sheet), cut a piece measuring 14¼X15⁵⁄₁₆". Now, lay out the top layer of the jig using the dimensions shown on the Jig Top Layer drawing *opposite, center*. Cut off the shaded areas. (We used a portable saber saw.)

5. Saw a second piece of ¾" particleboard to 16X19" for the jig's bottom layer. Place the top layer on the bottom layer. Align the longest edge of the top layer along one of the bottom layer's 19" edges. Locate the square corner of top layer 1¾" in from the nearest bottom corner. Nail the top to the bottom layer.

Assemble the basket

Note: *We predrilled the holes, and then used 1¼"X17 brads and Titebond II waterproof glue to assemble the basket, but the same work can be done in less time with a staple gun.*

1. Lay seven of the 5½" A pieces around the jig. (This will be the middle course.) Place the A piece with the ⅜" hole where shown on the Jig Top Layer drawing. Cut seven ¾X¾X2" cleats and nail them to the jig along the sides of the A pieces as shown in drawing A

2. Next, using the Planter Assembly drawing as a guide, begin at the outside tip and temporarily nail the second course of A pieces to the middle course. Let the nail heads extend ¼" above the surface. (After spacing the first A piece of the second course 1½" in from the basket tip, we angled it as shown, and then drilled pilot holes ⅜" in from each end. Then, as shown in drawing B, we drove the nails part way and attached the remaining pieces.)

3. Attach the remaining five courses, only this time glue each piece in place with Titebond II glue, and then drive the nails all the way.

4. When you have assembled the half-basket, remove the protruding nails from the second course as shown in drawing C, and separate it from the jig. Remove the middle course of A pieces, and pry off the cleats and the top layer of the jig.

Bill of Materials

Part	Finished Size T	W	L	Mat.	Qty.
A	¾"	¾"	5½"	R	49
B	¾"	¾"	16½"	R	1

Material Key: R—redwood
Supplies: 2—1½"-diameter metal rings, ⅜" rigid brass tubing, 1¼"X17 wire brads, waterproof glue.

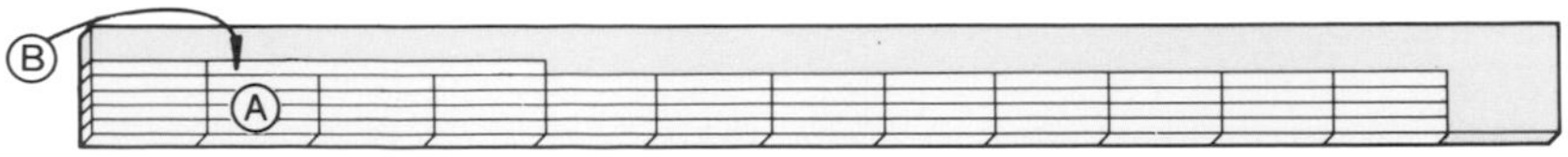

Cutting Diagram

¾X5½X72" Redwood

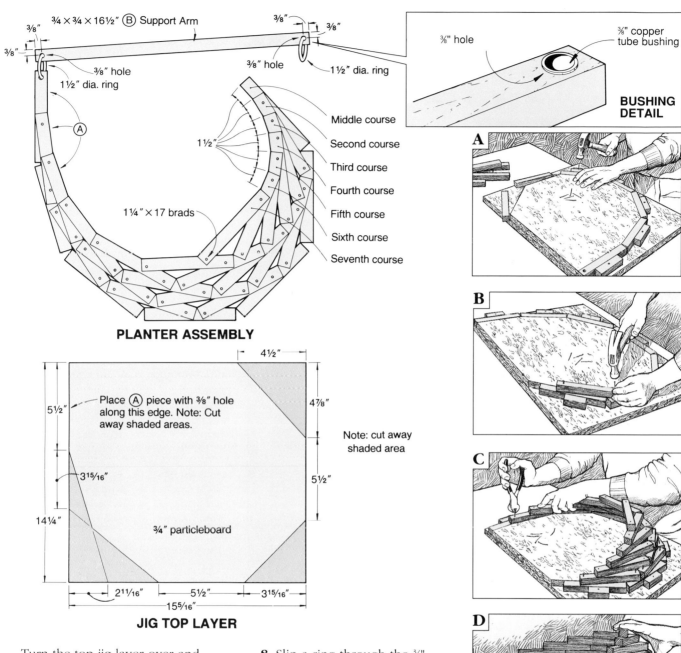

3/4 × 3/4 × 16 1/2" Ⓑ Support Arm

3/8" hole

1 1/2" dia. ring

3/8" hole

1 1/2" dia. ring

Ⓐ

1 1/2" dia. ring

3/8" hole

1 1/4" × 17 brads

Middle course

Second course

Third course

Fourth course

Fifth course

Sixth course

Seventh course

1 1/2"

PLANTER ASSEMBLY

3/8" hole

3/8" copper
tube bushing

**BUSHING
DETAIL**

A

B

C

D

4 1/2"

5 1/2"

4 7/8"

Place Ⓐ piece with 3/8" hole
along this edge. Note: Cut
away shaded areas.

Note: cut away
shaded area

3 15/16"

5 1/2"

14 1/4"

3/4" particleboard

2 11/16"   5 1/2"   3 15/16"

15 5/16"

JIG TOP LAYER

Turn the top jig layer over and reattach it to the bottom.

5. Assemble the second half of the basket, following the same assembly steps. This time, glue and nail the second course to the middle course. When assembled, remove this half-basket from the jig.

6. Align, and then glue and nail the two half-baskets together. (See drawing D.)

7. Secure the 1 1/2"-diameter metal rings in your vise (we used macrame rings) and cut through them at one point with a hacksaw. Spread the cut ends open with pliers.

8. Slip a ring through the 3/8" holes in the ends of support arm B. Next, fit one of the opened rings onto the basket to link it with the support. Pinch both rings to close them. Now, look for a place to hang your redwood planter.

Project Tool List
Tablesaw
Miter saw
Portable jigsaw
Portable drill
  3/8" bit

Note: We built the project using the tools listed. You may be able to substitute other tools or equipment for listed items you don't have. Additional common hand tools and clamps may be required to complete the project.

HEIRLOOM QUILT HANGER

Floor-model racks do a great job at displaying half a quilt. But if you seek the full effect, you're much better off with a wall-mounted quilt hanger. Made from cherry, our hanger features a unique pinch bar that holds the quilt firmly in place.

First, cut and shape the parts

1. Double the half-pattern on *page 22* by taping two pieces of 8½x11" typing paper together edge to edge. Next, fold the pieces at the tape joint, place carbon paper on top, and slip all three sheets beneath the pattern, aligning the taped edges of the paper with the *fold end* of the pattern. Trace the outline onto the top piece of paper, remove the carbon paper, and cut the traced pattern to shape. Next, cut out the inside half-oval for the decorative insert. Now, unfold the paper to make the full pattern. Save this and the piece you cut out for the insert.

2. To make the hanger back (A), rip and crosscut a piece of ¾" stock (we used cherry) to 5½x38". (See the Exploded View drawing.)

Note: We sized our hanger to match the display quilt shown at left. You can make your hanger to hold any size quilt you want by adding or subtracting length to the ends of back (A), and the pinch bar (C).

3. Center the paper pattern on the 5½"-wide piece, and align its bottom flush along one edge. Temporarily tape it in place, and trace the outline of the hanger's curved top onto the wood. If you want to include the decorative insert on your hanger, trace it at this time.

4. Using your tablesaw, start ripping the back piece to 2⅜" wide. Start from one end and rip to the point where the top curve starts. Stop there. Flip the piece end-to-end so the same edge remains against the fence, and rip toward the curve as shown in drawing A *below left.* Stop when you reach the curve again. Now, saw the curved area to shape on your bandsaw as shown in drawing B. Sand all surfaces. (We sanded the curve with a drum sander.)

5. Center and lock the back in a wood vise. Drill a ½" pilot hole in the area marked for the insert opening. Using a portable jigsaw, cut out the opening.

6. Chuck a 1"-diameter drum sander in your drill press. Sand inside of the opening. Next, chuck a ¼" piloted rabbeting bit in your router, and set it to cut ¼" deep.

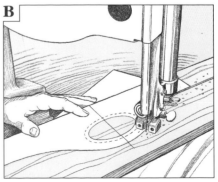

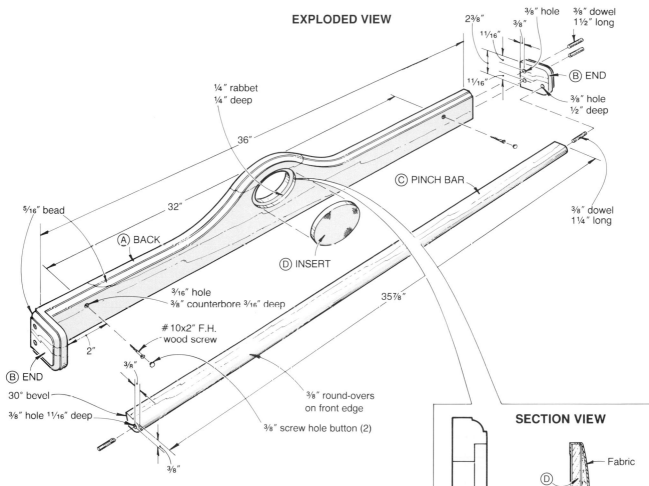

EXPLODED VIEW

2⅜"

3/8" hole

3/8" dowel 1½" long

11/16"

3/8"

Ⓑ END

11/16"

3/8" hole ½" deep

¼" rabbet ¼" deep

36"

Ⓒ PINCH BAR

3/8" dowel 1¼" long

5/16" bead

32"

Ⓐ BACK

Ⓓ INSERT

3/16" hole 3/8" counterbore 3/16" deep

35⅞"

#10x2" F.H. wood screw

2"

Ⓑ END

3/8"

30° bevel

3/8" hole 11/16" deep

3/8" round-overs on front edge

3/8" screw hole button (2)

3/8"

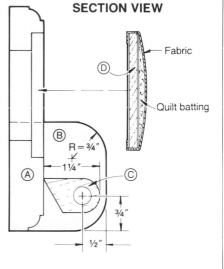

SECTION VIEW

Fabric

Ⓓ

Quilt batting

Ⓑ

R = ¾"

1¼"

Ⓐ

Ⓒ

¾"

½"

Rout the rabbet in the insert opening.

7. Rip a 12" length of ¾"-thick stock using the same saw setup used earlier in step 4.

8. Next, mark the ¾" radii on the four corners of the back. Saw the radii to shape; sand the edges. (We cut the corners with a bandsaw, and sanded them on a disc sander.)

9. Rout a 5/16" bead along the *front* edges on the back. Rout the same bead along the *top* edges and ends of the 12"-long piece.

10. Crosscut the back to final (36") length. (We measured 18" in both directions from the center and cut the back at those points.) Now, crosscut one 2⅛"-long end (B) from *each end* of the 12"-long piece.

11. To make the pinch bar (C), round over both edges on one side of a ¾"-thick piece at least 36" long. (We used a ⅜" round-over bit.) Next, set your tablesaw blade to

Bill of Materials					
Part	Finished Size*			Mat.	Qty.
	T	W	L		
A*	¾"	5"	36"	C	1
B	¾"	2⅜"	2⅛"	C	2
C	¾"	1¼"	35⅞"	C	1
D*	3/16"	3"	4½"	P	1

*Parts marked with an * are cut larger initially, and then trimmed to finished size. Please read the instructions carefully before cutting.

Material Key: C—cherry, P—plywood
Supplies: ⅜" dowel, 2—⅜" cherry screw-hole buttons, hotmelt glue, typing paper, carbon paper, 2—#10X1½" flathead wood screws, finish.

cut a 30° bevel; then, bevel-rip a 1¼"-wide piece as shown in drawing C on *page 23*. Now, crosscut the bar to 35⅞" length.

Next, do the drilling

1. First, cut four 1½" and two 1¼" lengths of ⅜" dowel.

2. Using dimensions on the Exploded View drawing, mark and drill the three dowel holes on the surfaces opposite the beaded edge. Back the pieces with scrap when drilling to prevent chip-out.

3. Mark and drill the dowel holes into the ends of the backpiece. (We held the end piece against the *continued*

HEIRLOOM QUILT HANGER
continued

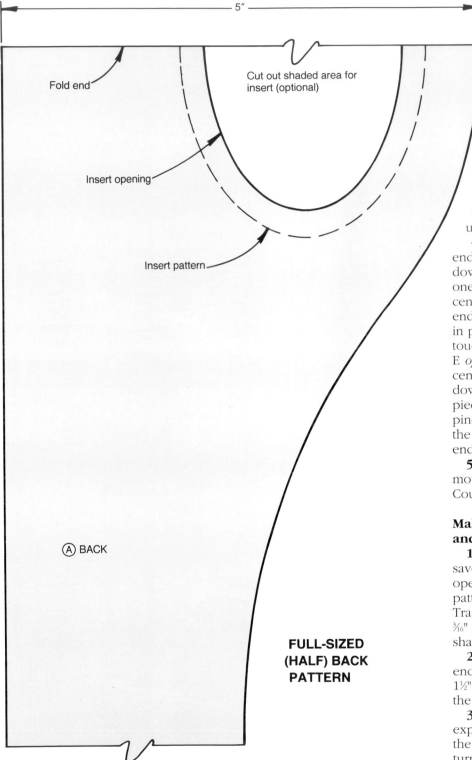

5"

Fold end

Cut out shaded area for insert (optional)

Insert opening

Insert pattern

Ⓐ BACK

FULL-SIZED (HALF) BACK PATTERN

hanger back and a fence to align.) Using a hand drill, insert a ⅜" bit through the drilled hole in the end piece and drill ⅞" deep into the back piece. Temporarily insert a 3" length of ⅜" dowel through the hole in the end piece and into the back. Next, drill the second hole in the end of the back as shown in drawing D, *opposite*. Remove the dowel. Drill the holes on the opposite end of the back using the same technique.

4. To locate the ⅜" holes in the ends of the pinch bar, place a ⅜" dowel center in the front hole of one of the end pieces. Strike a centerline the long way on both ends of the pinch bar. Hold the bar in position so the beveled edge touches the back piece as shown in E *opposite*. Now, align the centerline with the point of the dowel center, and press the end piece and dowel center against the pinch bar. Mark the other end. Drill the two ⅜" holes, ¹¹⁄₁₆" deep in the ends of the bar.

5. Mark and drill the two ³⁄₁₆" mounting holes in the hanger back. Counterbore the holes ³⁄₁₆" deep.

Make the insert; then, assemble and finish the hanger

1. Tape the insert cutout you saved earlier back into the pattern opening. Now, cut out the insert pattern following the dashed line. Trace the pattern onto a piece of ³⁄₁₆" plywood scrap. Cut the insert to shape.

2. Glue a 1¼"-long dowel in the ends of the pinch bar, and two 1½"-long dowels in the ends of the back.

3. Once the glue dries, sand the exposed portion of the dowels in the ends of the pinch bar so they'll turn easily in the ⅜" holes.

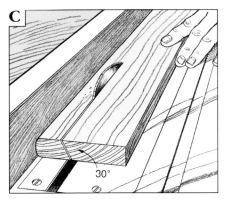

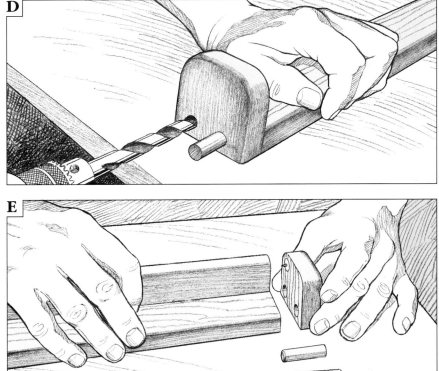

4. Apply glue to the dowels on one end of the back and slide one end over them until it butts tight against the back. Next, glue the dowels on the opposite end and start them into the holes in the end piece but *do not* push the piece all the way on. Now, insert the dowel in the end of the pinch bar into the hole in the end already in place. Finally, align the dowel at the other end with the hole in the end piece; then, push this end into place. Clamp the assembly.

5. Sand the dowels exposed on the ends flush. Sand the squeeze bar.

6. Finish the quilt hanger. (We applied three coats of spray lacquer, sanding each coat with 320-grit sandpaper after it dried.)

7. Cover the insert piece as desired, and place it in the opening. (We created the decorative star on fabric, and backed it with quilt batting as shown in the Section View on the Exploded View drawing on *page 21.* Then, we applied four spots of hotmelt glue to hold the insert in the opening.)

8. Mount the hanger level on the wall with flathead screws or hollow wall anchors. Finally, glue the screw-hole buttons in place.

Project Tool List
Tablesaw
Bandsaw
Portable jigsaw
Portable drill
Drill press
   1" drum sander
   Bits: ³⁄₁₆", ⅜"
Router
   Bits: ¼" rabbet, ⁵⁄₁₆" bead,
     ⅜" round-over
Disc sander
Finishing sander

Note: We built the project using the tools listed. You may be able to substitute other tools or equipment for listed items you don't have. Additional common hand tools and clamps may be required to complete the project.

BOOK OF MEMORIES

measuring 13½" for the front (A), and two 11¼" lengths for the sides (B). (See the Cutting Diagram *below* for help in laying out the pieces.)

2. Using the dimensions on the Sides and Front drawing *below*, rout a rabbet (we used a ½"-straight bit) along both ends of the front piece. Cut a 13½" length of scrap and temporarily nail it to the ends of each side. Next, apply glue (we used yellow woodworker's glue) to the rabbets of the front piece and join them with the ends of the side pieces to complete the box frame. Now, align the edges, square the corners, and clamp.

3. Install a 1⁄16"-thick plywood blade in your tablesaw and elevate it to 1⁄16" above the table. With a square placed against the blade, strike a pencil line perpendicular to the blade on the saw table surface and to the right side. Starting at the blade, place a mark 1⁄16" from the blade. Next, make 24 marks, one every 1⁄8" from this mark

The next time you shop for a photo album, check its quality. You'll find most made of plastic-covered cardboard. If your family photos deserve better, then picture them in this leather-bound oak album. It's the perfect coffee-table centerpiece and a project your family will cherish for years.

Note: Before starting the album, buy a standard 3-ring binder measuring 1½" wide and 11" long, with 2½"-diameter rings. With a hacksaw blade, cut the rivets that hold the binder to the cardboard backing.

First, make the book front and sides

1. Rip and crosscut a piece of ¾" stock (we used oak) to 3×40". Plane or resaw the piece to ½" thickness. From it, cut one length

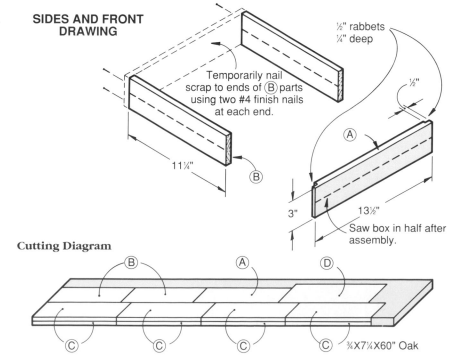

SIDES AND FRONT DRAWING

½" rabbets
¼" deep

Temporarily nail scrap to ends of (B) parts using two #4 finish nails at each end.

½"

(A)

11¼"

(B)

3"

13½"

Saw box in half after assembly.

Cutting Diagram

(B) (A) (D)

(C) (C) (C) (C) ¾X7¼X60" Oak

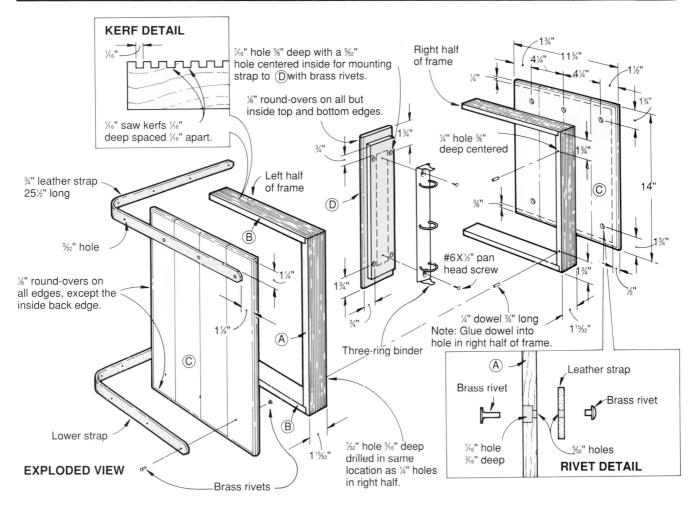

KERF DETAIL

1⁄16"

1⁄16" saw kerfs 1⁄16" deep spaced 1⁄16" apart.

7⁄16" hole 5⁄8" deep with a 5⁄32" hole centered inside for mounting strap to Ⓓ with brass rivets.

1⁄8" round-overs on all but inside top and bottom edges.

Right half of frame

Left half of frame

Ⓑ

3⁄4" leather strap 25½" long

5⁄32" hole

1⁄8" round-overs on all edges, except the inside back edge.

1¼"

 Ⓐ

1¼"

Ⓒ

Lower strap

EXPLODED VIEW

Brass rivets

3⁄4"

1¾"

Ⓓ

1¾"

3⁄4"

1⁄4" hole 3⁄8" deep centered

#6 X ½" pan head screw

1⁄4" dowel 3⁄4" long
Note: Glue dowel into hole in right half of frame.

Three-ring binder

7⁄32" hole 5⁄16" deep drilled in same location as 1⁄4" holes in right half.

1¾"
4¼"
11¾"
1⁄4"
4¼"
1½"
1¾"
1¾"

3⁄8"

Ⓒ

14"

1¾"

1¾"

1¾"
1½"
1 15⁄32"
½"

ⓐ
Brass rivet
Leather strap
Brass rivet

7⁄16" hole 3⁄16" deep

5⁄32" holes

RIVET DETAIL

Bill of Materials				
Part	Finished Size		Mat.	Qty.
	T	W	L		
A front	½"	3"	13½"	O	1
B sides	½"	3"	11¼"	O	2
C covers	5⁄16"	11¾"	14"	O	2
D back	3⁄4"	3½"	14"	O	1

Material Key: O—Oak.
Supplies: Gold enamel paint, small brush, 3-ring binder, 2—#6 X ½" panhead screws, stain, polyurethane finish, album filler pages.

along the line. Now, lock the rip fence at the 1⁄16" mark.

4. To simulate the look of book pages (see Kerf detail *above*), place the frame against the fence, turn on the saw, and, as shown at *right*, saw a kerf along the sides and front. Stop the saw, move the fence to the next mark, and saw a second kerf. Now, using the marks as guides, saw kerfs along both sides and the front.

5. Raise the blade to 5⁄8", lock the fence 17⁄16" from the blade, and cut the frame in two lengthwise, including the temporary scrap end.

6. Measure in 1¾" from both front corners along the top front edge of the right half frame, and mark the centerpoints for two 1⁄4" holes. (See the Exploded View drawing *above.*)

Drill these holes 3⁄8" deep on your drill press, clamping the frame to prevent movement. Next, place 1⁄4" dowel centers in these holes. Put the mating left half frame on top of the right half frame, align the edges, and then press them together to mark the locations for the mating holes in the left half frame. Now, drill the two newly marked 7⁄32" holes 5⁄16" deep.

7. Cut two 5⁄8" lengths of 1⁄4" dowel and bevel-sand the ends. Apply glue in the 1⁄4" holes you drilled in the edges of the bottom side piece in step 6. Insert the dowels, allowing 1⁄4" to protrude. Test the fit by joining the two half frames together.

8. Finish-sand the edges and kerfs to remove saw marks and splinters. (When sanding the side kerfs, we double-folded a piece of 150-grit sandpaper and worked the folded edge through each kerf.)

continued

BOOK OF MEMORIES
continued

9. Apply masking tape to both edges of each frame half. Brush a fast-drying gold enamel paint on the kerfed surfaces. After it dries, apply a second paint coat. Let that paint dry and remove the tape.

Now, make and attach the covers

1. Rip and crosscut a piece of ¾" oak to 3x60". Resaw the piece in half with a ⅛"-thick carbide-tipped blade to get two ⁵⁄₁₆"-thick lengths. (We used our tablesaw with the blade elevated to 1¾", sawed along one edge, turned the piece over and end for end, and then sawed through the remaining half.) Sand away all the saw marks.

2. Place a pencil mark along the length of one piece. Crosscut both ⁵⁄₁₆" pieces into four 15" lengths. For matching grain, dry-assemble the marked pieces as one panel, the unmarked ones as the second. Edge-join the panels with glue and clamp.

3. Scrape any glue squeeze-out from the panel joints and sand away the saw marks. Now, rip and crosscut the panels to make a front and back covers (C), using the dimensions listed in the Bill of Materials on *page 25*.

4. With a ⅛" round-over bit, rout along all but the back inside edges of both covers.

5. To glue the frames to the covers, place the right frame inside face down on your bench. Apply a bead of glue along the three edges of the frame (see the Exploded View drawing on *page 25*). Next, lay the back cover on top of the frame, aligning the unrounded edge with the back of the frame. Allow ¼" overhang on the sides and front. Clamp the parts together at each corner. Now, assemble the left frame and cover the same way.

6. After the glue dries, carefully remove the scrap pine pieces attached to the ends of each frame half.

Make the book's back

1. For the book's back (D), rip and crosscut a piece of ¾" oak to the dimensions listed in the Bill of Materials.

2. Rout the ⅜" and ¾" rabbets ½" deep on the back piece where shown on the Book Back drawing *below*. Next, switch back to the ⅛" round-over bit you used earlier, and rout a round-over along the outside edges and the two long edges on the inside. (See the Exploded View drawing.)

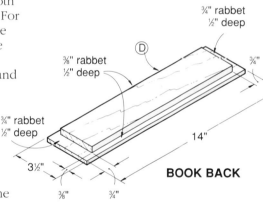

⅜" rabbet ½" deep
¾" rabbet ½" deep
¾" rabbet ½" deep
D
¾"
14"
3½"
⅜"
¾"

BOOK BACK

Add the letters, finish, and then assemble

1. Finish-sand all but the painted kerfs on the sides and front. For uniform staining of both end grain and flat surfaces, apply paste wood filler, following label directions. Wipe off the residue. Next, apply a stain and let it dry. (We applied a golden-oak stain.)

2. Lightly finish-sand the unpainted album parts. Position the letter on the cover. (We used ¾" laser-cut walnut letters for "THE" and "ALBUM," and 1" letters for the family name and the word "FAMILY." See our Buying Guide *opposite* for a mail-order source, or

paint the letters if you like.) Mark the letter locations, and then glue each in place. Weight the letters with a piece of plywood until the glue dries.

3. Erase pencil marks and remove any glue squeeze-out. apply the final finish to all surfaces. (We applied two coats of poly- urethane, sanding with 320-grit sandpaper between coats.)

4. Cut two ⅛x¾x25½" leather straps for hinges, using a sharp utility knife and straightedge. (We purchased our leather supplies from a local Tandy leather store. See the Buying Guide to mail order.) Trim the ends of each strap. Apply the dye to the straps and let it dry. Finally, apply a sheen leather finish.

5. Lay the straps across the outside face of the back and 1¼" in from the ends. Allow the same length of strap to extend beyond each edge. Chuck a ⁵⁄₃₂" brad-point bit in your drill press and drill two holes through each strap and the back where shown on the Exploded View drawing. Set the straps aside, flip the back over, change to a ⁷⁄₁₆" drill bit, and drill ⅝"-deep holes at the ⁵⁄₃₂" hole locations.

6. Insert the shaft of a ½"-long brass rivet through one of the back holes from the inside. Place a strap over the shaft at the appropriate hole location. (You'll need two inexpensive rivet tools, and a helper to hold the back horizontal while seating the rivet head.) Next, have your helper place the flat end of one rivet tool against the flat bottom of the rivet shaft and the other end on a hard surface. Press the rivet head onto the rivet shaft, fit the concave end of the second rivet tool over the head and strike the tool with a hammer to seat the head. Seat the other three rivets.

7. Temporarily assemble the album. Position one strap where

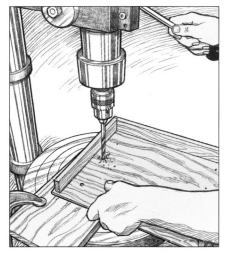

shown on the Exploded View drawing and pull it tight. Following the hole measurements, mark and drill through the strap and cover as shown *above*. (We inserted finish nails through the drilled holes to keep the straps tight.) Locate the holes for the second strap the same way. Counterbore the holes on the inside of the covers following the Rivet detail on the Exploded View drawing, and as shown *below*.

8. Again, with a helper (see illustration *above*), follow the process described in step 6 and rivet the leather straps to secure the covers.

9. Locate and drill small pilot holes for the #6x½" panhead screws that hold the three-ring binder mechanism to the back. Screw the binder to the back. Now, start adding pages of beloved family photos. (We purchased 3-ring photograph album filler pages locally.)

Buying Guide
•**Leather supplies.** ProDye (dark brown), #2055, 4 oz. container; Super Shene, #2002, 4 oz. container, daubers, #1829; rivets (long, brass), #1275; 2-rivet tools, #8100; leather strip, 1x60", #4591. For current prices, contact Tandy Leather Company, P.O. Box 2934, Fort Worth, TX 76113.

•**Walnut letters.** ¾" tall, 1" tall. For current prices, contact Paddle Tramps Mfg. Co., 1317 University Ave., Lubbock, TX 79401, or call 806-765-9901.

Project Tool List
Tablesaw
Drill press
   Bits: ⁵⁄₃₂", ⁷⁄₁₆", ⁷⁄₃₂", ¼"
Router
   Bits: ½" straight, ⅜" rabbet,
    ¾" rabbet, ⅛" round-over
Finishing sander

Note: *We built the project using the tools listed. You may be able to substitute other tools or equipment for listed items you don't have. Additional common hand tools and clamps may be required to complete the project.*

FROM THE DESK OF...

Everyone appreciates the warmth that wood desk accessories bring to the office. You can select from a variety of projects here to put together the perfect gift for the executive.

LAMINATED LETTER OPENER

Short on gifts but long on scrap? If so, you'll find our hardwood opener, with its interesting chevron-patterned handle, a real lifesaver. It's hard to believe that something so simple could be so elegant.

1. From ¾" stock, cut the strips for the handle lamination (A, B, C, D) to the sizes listed in the Bill of Materials. (We specified 11" lengths for these pieces to allow for safety when miter-cutting the lamination.) There's enough length to the lamination to cut handle pieces for several additional openers.

2. Glue and clamp the strips together stair-step fashion in the sequence shown in the Handle Lamination drawing *below.* Keep the top edges of all the strips flush when clamping. After the glue dries, remove the clamps, and scrape off the excess glue. Belt-sand the top and bottom surfaces smooth.

3. Position your radial arm saw blade to cut a 45° angle, and mitercut one end of the lamination where shown on the Handle Lamination drawing. Now, mark a stop line on the saw table to ensure consistent ½"-wide miter cuts (see the photo *top right*). Cut the number of handle strips desired.

4. Cut the oak blade (E) to size.

5. Glue and clamp the handle pieces to the blade. Align the pieces so they create the pattern shown in the full-sized Top View drawing on *page 30.*

6. Using carbon paper, transfer the Top View of the handle and Side View of the blade to cardboard. (We used the back from a writing tablet.) Cut the cardboard templates to shape. Trace the handle outline onto the top of the handle and the blade outline onto the side of the oak blade. Cut the handle and blade to shape on a bandsaw as shown in the photo *below, center.*

continued

Mark a stop line on the table for consistent lamination lengths. Miter the handle pieces on the radial arm saw.

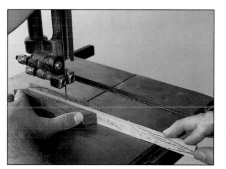

Cut the letter opener handle and blade to shape on a bandsaw fitted with a fine-tooth blade.

Bill of Materials

Part	Initial size			Mat.	Qty.
	T	W	L		
A	¾"	¼"	11"	C	4
B	¾"	¼"	11"	W	2
C	¾"	1½"	11"	W	1
D	¾"	1¼"	11"	W	1
E	¾"	5⁄16"	12"	O	1

Material Key: C—cardinal wood, W—walnut, O—oak
Supplies: Watco Danish oil, #0000 steel wool.

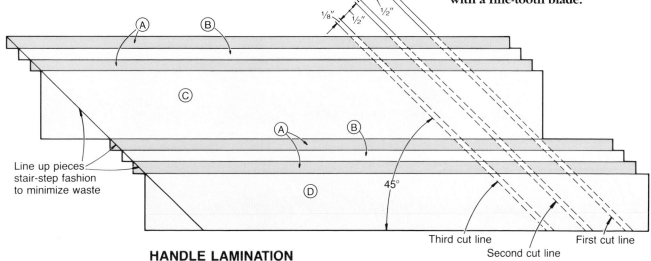

Line up pieces stair-step fashion to minimize waste

⅛"
⅛"
⅛"
½"
½"
45°
Third cut line
Second cut line
First cut line

HANDLE LAMINATION

LAMINATED LETTER OPENER
continued

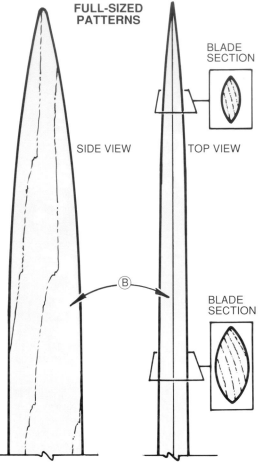

FULL-SIZED PATTERNS

SIDE VIEW

BLADE SECTION

TOP VIEW

Connect the dividing lines from the bottom of the pieces on the left to the top of the pieces on the right for a complete pattern

BLADE SECTION

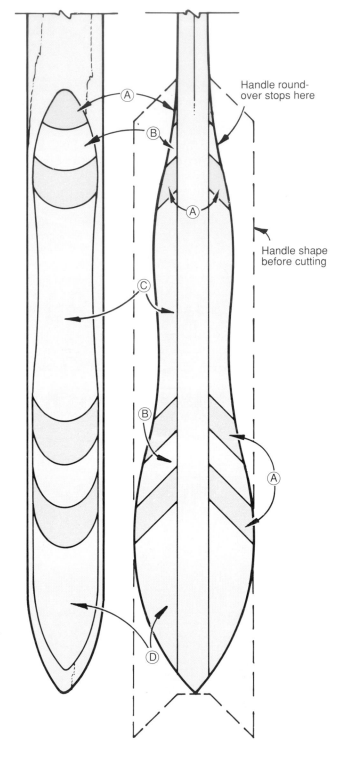

Handle round-over stops here

Handle shape before cutting

7. Rout a round-over on all edges of the handle, stopping where shown on the full-sized Top View. (We used a ⅜" round-over bit chucked into our table-mounted router.)

8. Using the blade pattern on the Side View as a guide, sand the blade to shape (we used a belt sander; a drum sander would also work well). When sanding, bevel both edges of the blade to the shape shown in the Blade Sections accompanying the full-sized Top View.

9. Finish-sand the completed letter opener.

10. Finish as desired. (We applied several coats of Watco Danish Oil, rubbing lightly between coats with #0000 steel wool.)

Note: *After opening a few hundred letters, you may need to "sharpen" the blade. To do so, sand with a belt sander or drum sander; and then refinish the blade.*

Project Tool List
Tablesaw
Radial arm saw
Bandsaw
Belt sander
Router
    Router table
    ⅜" round-over bit

Note: *We built the project using the tools listed. You may be able to substitute other tools or equipment for listed items you don't have. Additional common hand tools and clamps may be required to complete the project.*

THE MINI-SAFE AND BILL BOX OR KEY KEEPER

Kids will love saving for tomorrow in an oak safe highlighting one of yesteryear's treasures—a genuine brass lockbox door. The restored brass door—salvaged from one of America's post offices—comes complete with a working combination. Refurbished post office lockbox doors add just the right amount of nostalgia to

these handsomely useful projects.

Staying organized in this day and age isn't easy. But with the bill box and key keeper you'll at least know the whereabouts of those ever-present bills, and be able to keep track of otherwise-elusive car keys that always seem to wander off.

First, make a basic box for the mini-safe

1. Cut a piece of ½"-thick oak to 4" wide by 24" long. Cut or rout a ¼" groove ¼" deep and ¼" from one edge of the oak strip.

2. Tilt your table saw blade 45° from center. Using a miter gauge fitted with a fence, miter-cut the sides (A) and top and bottom (B) to length from the 24"-long strip.

3. Using the dimensions on the drawing, mark the slot on the top face of the top piece (B). Drill a ¼" hole at each end of the slot. Using a ³⁄₁₆" bit, drill out the waste material between the two ¼" holes. Then, chisel the slot to shape, or cut it to shape with a scrollsaw.

4. Cut the box back (C) to size from ¼" oak or lauan plywood.

5. Glue and clamp the box assembly together. (We used masking tape to hold the mitered joints together, and then pulled the joints tight with a band clamp.)

Add a base

1. Cut a piece of ½"-thick oak to ¾" wide by 24" long. Miter-cut the base pieces (D, E) to length from the strip. Mark the opening on the four pieces to form the feet where shown on the Exploded View drawing on *page 32*.

2. Cut the base pieces to shape. (We cut ours on a bandsaw fitted with a ⅛" blade.) Sand the rounded corners smooth with a 1"-diameter drum sander.

Putting it all together

1. Glue and clamp the base pieces to the bottom of the box.

2. Position the door and drill ⅜"-deep holes in the opening. The holes will be slightly angled.

3. Sand the assembly smooth. Stain and finish as desired. Screw the door in place. Then, empty your pocket change into the bank.

continued

THE MINI-SAFE AND BILL BOX OR KEY KEEPER
continued

Cut and assemble the letter box

1. Rip and crosscut the back (A), front (B), two sides (C), shelf (D), and bottom (E) to the sizes listed in the Bill of Materials on *page 33*.

2. Mark and cut a 2¼" radius on the top of the back piece. Rout a ⅜" round-over on the top back edge of the front piece.

3. Using a try square, mark the door-opening location on the front piece, and cut it to shape. Check the fit of the door in the opening.

4. Using double-faced tape, fasten the two side pieces (C)

together face to face with the edges flush. Mark a 2¾" radius on one piece where dimensioned on the drawing, and cut and sand both pieces to shape. Remove the tape.

5. Mark the location, and cut a ½" rabbet ¼" deep along the bottom edge of the back (A). Using the dimensions on the drawing, mark the locations and cut a ½" dado ¼" deep in the front and back pieces. Check the fit of the shelf and bottom in the dadoes and rabbet.

6. Mark the location and drill pilot holes for the two cup hooks

and two mounting holes for attaching the box to the wall after assembly.

7. With the bottom edges of the sides and back flush, glue and clamp them together. (We positioned the shelf and bottom in place to hold the assembly square.) Glue and clamp the shelf, bottom, and front to the assembly.

8. Transfer the eagle pattern *opposite* to ¼" oak stock, and cut it to shape. (We planed down a piece of ½" stock for the ¼"-thick eagle.)

Bill of Materials

Part	Finished Size*			Mat.	Qty
	T	**W**	**L**		
A* sides	½"	4"	5½"	O	2
B* top & bottom	½"	4"	4³⁄₁₆"	O	2
C back	¼"	3⅝"	4¹⁵⁄₁₆"	OP	1
D* base	½"	¾"	4³⁄₁₆"	O	2
E* base	½"	¾"	4"	O	2

*Parts marked with an * are cut larger initially and then trimmed to finished size. Please read the instructions carefully before cutting.

Material Key: O—oak, OP—oak plywood
Supplies: #4X⅜" flathead wood screws, stain, finish.

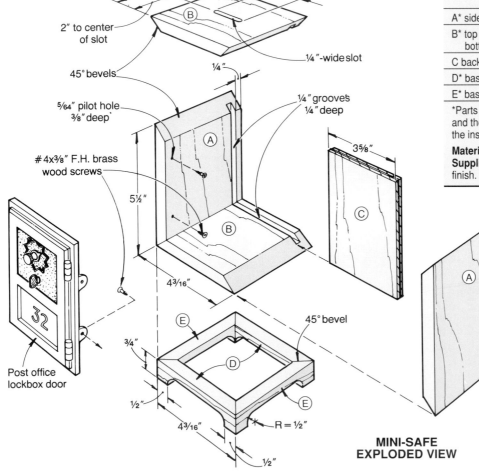

MINI-SAFE EXPLODED VIEW

Now, mount the door and add the finish

1. Sand the box smooth. Hold the bronze door in place, and drill the angled pilot holes in the opening in the front piece. Remove the door.

2. Stain and finish the box. Mount the door and hang the box, centering it over a stud if possible.

Note: If you don't want to use the combination each time you open the door, remove the lock mechanism from the back of the door. Then, remount the dial.

Buying Guide
• Post office lockbox door.
Grecian style with two-digit decal. Reconditioned doors shipped with three-letter combination. For current prices, contact Streeter Company, P.O. Box 241, Sturgeon, MO 65284, or call 314-687-3311.

Project Tool List
Tablesaw
   Dado blade or dado set
Scrollsaw
Bandsaw
Portable drill
   1" drum sander
   Bits: ⅟₁₆", ⅝₄", ³⁄₁₆", ¼"
Router
   Router table
   Bits: ½" straight, ⅜" round-over
Finishing sander

Note: We built the project using the tools listed. You may be able to substitute other tools or equipment for listed items you don't have. Additional common hand tools and clamps may be required to complete the project.

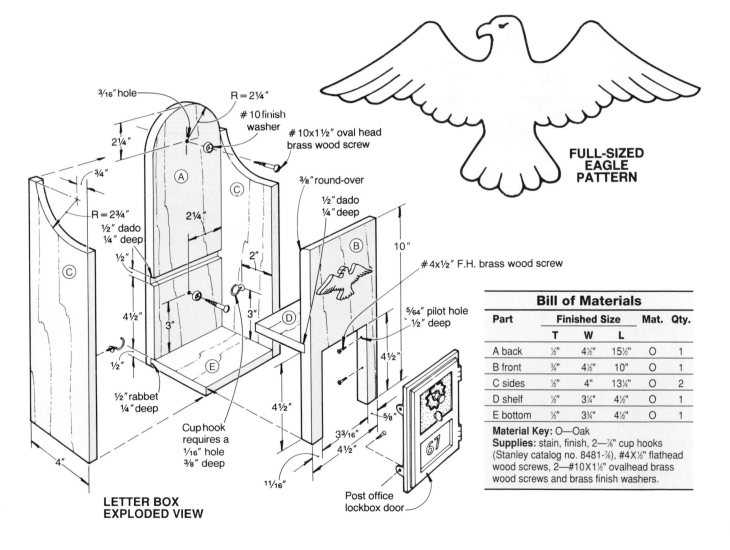

FULL-SIZED EAGLE PATTERN

LETTER BOX EXPLODED VIEW

Post office lockbox door

Bill of Materials

Part	Finished Size			Mat.	Qty.
	T	W	L		
A back	½"	4½"	15½"	O	1
B front	¾"	4½"	10"	O	1
C sides	½"	4"	13¼"	O	2
D shelf	½"	3¼"	4½"	O	1
E bottom	½"	3¾"	4½"	O	1

Material Key: O—Oak
Supplies: stain, finish, 2—⅞" cup hooks (Stanley catalog no. 8481-⅞), #4X½" flathead wood screws, 2—#10X1½" ovalhead brass wood screws and brass finish washers.

EXECUTIVE PAPERWEIGHT

How many times have you stashed away a small block of beautifully grained wood waiting for just the right opportunity to use it? Well, here's the project you've been yearning for. You'll want to make several of these distinguished-looking creations to have on hand for those special gift-giving occasions.

Note, we turned one from walnut, another from spalted maple, and one from a lamination.

Readying the stock

1. Select a block of wood measuring approximately 4¼" square by 3" thick If you don't have stock this thick, laminate thinner stock.

2. On the bottom of the block—the 4¼"-square surface—draw diagonals to find its center. Using a compass and the centerpoint that you've just located, draw a 4"-diameter circle. Saw the block to shape with a bandsaw, cutting just outside the marked circle.

3. Drill a ¾" hole 1½" deep at the 4" circle centerpoint. (The hole will give you a depth reference, making it easier to turn the washer recess to size later.)

4. Cut a 4"-diameter disc from ¾" plywood scrap. Center and screw it to a faceplate to form an auxiliary faceplate. Center, and glue and clamp the *top* surface of the cylinder (opposite the end with the ¾" hole) to the auxiliary faceplate. (We used a glue and paper joint between the two.)

Let's start turning

Note: *The turning process involves two basic steps. First, mount the cylinder to the lathe, square the bottom, and turn the 1⅜" hole and plug recess to size. Next, you remount the plugged and weighted cylinder and turn it to shape.*

1. Mount the faceplate-cylinder assembly to your lathe, and set the lathe speed to about 800 rpm. With a ⅜" or ½" gouge, rough-turn the blank until it's perfectly cylindrical. Square up the bottom as shown in the Exploded View drawing *opposite, top.*

2. Enlarge the ¾" hole you drilled earlier to 1⅜" (we used a parting tool). The hole should be just wide enough to accept 1⅜"-outside diameter washers, which you'll use to add weight to the paperweight. With a parting tool or skew, form a 2"-wide recess ¼" deep to house the plug as shown in drawing A *opposite.*

3. Remove the assembly from the lathe, and separate the cylinder

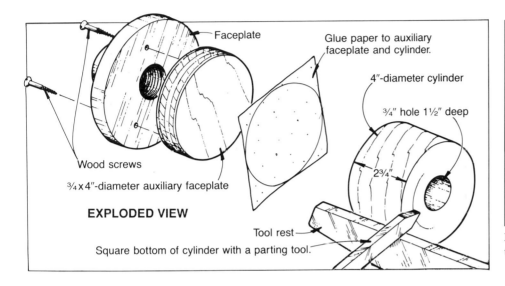

Faceplate

Glue paper to auxiliary faceplate and cylinder.

4"-diameter cylinder

¾" hole 1½" deep

2¾"

Wood screws

¾ x 4"-diameter auxiliary faceplate

EXPLODED VIEW

Tool rest

Square bottom of cylinder with a parting tool.

Parting the paperweight from the lathe

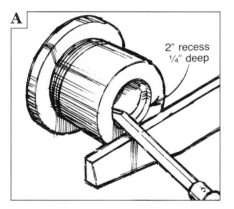

A

2" recess ¼" deep

from the auxiliary faceplate by breaking the paper-glue joint with a chisel. Sand or turn the auxiliary faceplate smooth for good adhesion to the plug blank in the next step.

4. To fashion the plug for the bottom of the paperweight, cut a 2¼"-diameter disc from a piece of ¾" stock. You can use the same kind of wood as the paperweight or one of a contrasting color. Center and glue the disc to the auxiliary faceplate, and mount it to your lathe. Use a skew to form a plug from the disc to fit snugly in the recess. (When turning the plug to size, we stopped the lathe periodically to check the fit).

5. Lay the turned cylinder on a flat surface with the hole facing up. Insert flat washers in the 1⅜" hole (or fill with lead shot) for weight. Mix the epoxy (we used slow-set), and pour it into the 1⅜" washer-filled hole. Epoxy the plug (still mounted to the faceplate) into the ¼"-deep recess.

6. After the epoxy has cured (24 hours in our case), remount the faceplate and cylinder to the lathe. Turn the cylinder to shape using drawing B *below* as a reference. Adjust the lathe speed to about

B

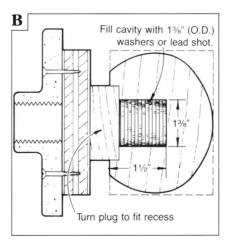

Fill cavity with 1⅜" (O.D.) washers or lead shot.

1⅜"

1½"

Turn plug to fit recess

1,200 rpm, sand the paperweight smooth, and apply the finish (we used an oil finish).

7. With a parting tool, cut a groove about ½" deep in the plug stock, flush with the bottom of the paperweight, as shown in the photo *above*. Stop the lathe, and use a backsaw to cut through the rest of the plug, being careful not to let the paperweight fall.

Project Tool List
Bandsaw
Drill press
  ¾" bit
Lathe
  3-4" faceplate
  ⅜", ½" gouges
  ⅛" parting tool
  ½" skew

Note: *We built the project using the tools listed. You may be able to substitute other tools or equipment for listed items you don't have. Additional common hand tools and clamps may be required to complete the project.*

TAKING CARE OF BUSINESS CARD CASE

Closed for carrying

Fully opened for display

Carry your business cards with pride using this beautiful project. Back at your desk, flip the card case open and display your calling cards as shown *above right*. We used morado for our case, but most any hardwood will do. Just take your time and search your scrap bin for the stock with the most dramatic grain.

Note: You'll need some ⅛" stock for this project. You can plane or resaw thicker stock to size. After planing or resawing your own stock, let it sit a couple of days to see if it cups. The stock you use must remain flat.

Also, business cards vary in size. We built our holder for a 2⅛×3" card. Adjust the size of the holder to fit your cards.

Cut the parts and glue 'em together

1. Cut the lid hinge parts (A), top (B), tray front and back (C), tray bottom (D), and tray sides (E) to the sizes listed in the Bill of Materials. (We cut the pieces on our tablesaw using a thin-kerf blade.) See the Cutting Diagram for minimum waste. (We found it safer to cut the narrow parts first. Also, we clamped a stop on our radial-arm saw fence to ensure consistent lengths of parts A, B, C, and D.)

2. With the edges and ends flush, glue the lid-hinge parts (A) together face to face. (For ease and quickness of assembly of such small parts, we used gap-filling cyano-acrylate adhesive—instant glue—to bond the parts. Cyanoacrylate is available at most hobby shops. To clamp the tiny lid-hinge parts together, we used ordinary wooden clothespins.)

3. To form the lid, glue the lid hinge (A) flush with the back edge and ends of the lid top (B).

4. To form the tray, glue the front and back pieces (C) to the tray bottom (D). Keep the ends flush. Then, glue the tray sides (E) to the tray assembly.

Pinning the lid to the tray

1. Using the Hole detail at *far right* for reference, mark the hinge-pin centerpoint on both ends of the tray sides. Using an awl or nail, make a slight indentation at each marked centerpoint. The indentation will keep the drill bit from wandering in the next step.

2. Using masking tape, fasten the lid to the tray with the edges and ends flush. Lightly clamp the assembly in a handscrew clamp as shown in the photo *opposite*. Chuck a ¹⁄₁₆" bit into your drill press, and

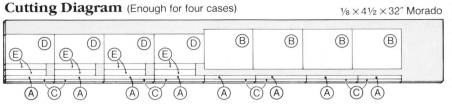

Tablesaw
Radial arm saw
Drill press
   $\frac{1}{16}''$ bit
Finishing sander

Note: *We built the project using the tools listed. You may be able to substitute other tools or equipment for listed items you don't have. Additional common hand tools and clamps may be required to complete the project.*

Part	Finished Size			Mat.	Qty.
	T	**W**	**L**		
A lid hinge	$\frac{1}{4}''$	$\frac{5}{16}''$	$3\frac{5}{8}''$	LM	1
B lid top	$\frac{1}{8}''$	3"	$3\frac{5}{8}''$	M	1
C tray back & front	$\frac{1}{8}''$	$\frac{3}{16}''$	$3\frac{5}{8}''$	M	2
D tray bottom	$\frac{1}{8}''$	$2\frac{1}{2}''$	$3\frac{5}{8}''$	M	1
E tray slides	$\frac{1}{8}''$	$\frac{7}{16}''$	3"	M	2

Material Key: LM—laminated morado,
            M—morado
Supplies: $\frac{1}{16}''$ brass rod, finish.

position the tray/lid assembly so the bit aligns directly over the indented hinge-pin centerpoint on the tray side. Drill a $\frac{1}{16}''$ hole $\frac{1}{2}''$ deep in both ends of the holder as shown in the photo *below*.

Mark the location of the hinge pins, tape the assemblies together with the edges and ends flush, and drill $\frac{1}{16}''$ holes.

3. Cut two pieces of $\frac{1}{16}''$ brass rod to $\frac{5}{16}''$ long.

4. Remove the tape to separate the lid from the tray. Using the pointed end of a pin or toothpick, put a small amount of instant glue into each $\frac{1}{16}''$ hole in the lid hinge (A). Insert the pins through tray sides (E) and into the lid hinge to pin the lid to the tray sides. Sand the ends of the brass pins flush with the surface of the sides.

Add the finger recess, round-overs, and finish

1. Sand all surfaces and ends flush. Close the lid, and sand or rout $\frac{1}{8}''$ round-overs along the outside edges of the case.

2. Measure in $1\frac{5}{8}''$ from the inside surface of both E's, and mark a pair of lines on the tray front (C) to locate the finger recess where shown on the Exploded View drawing *below*. Wrap 150-grit sandpaper around a $\frac{3}{8}''$ dowel, and sand between the lines to form the finger recess. (The size of the recess depends on personal preference. For those with small fingers, a shallow recess was sufficient. We recommend a deeper and wider recess for someone with larger fingers.)

3. Finish-sand the holder (inside and out) and apply the finish of your choice, rubbing lightly with steel wool between coats. To help prevent warping, apply an equal number of coats to the inside and outside surfaces.

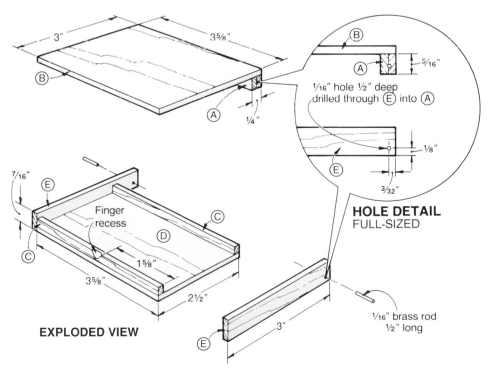

EXPLODED VIEW

HOLE DETAIL
FULL-SIZED

READY-REFERENCE CALENDAR/CLOCK

We liked this digital calendar/clock so much that we built an attractive oak stand to go with it. And, the alarm feature makes this project suitable for the bedroom, office, or any other room where busy people plan their day.

Cut the pieces, and form the groove

1. Cut the 3×3¾" base piece to size from ¾"-thick stock. Sand it smooth. From the same ¾" stock, cut a piece 4×12" for the slanted back. (For safe machining, we began with an extra-long piece.)

2. Referring to the three-step drawing shown *below*, cut a groove down the center, and then bevel-rip both edges of the back.

3. Sand the back smooth. (We wrapped sandpaper around a scrap block to sand the grooved area.) Sand a slight round-over

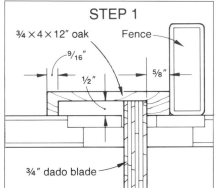

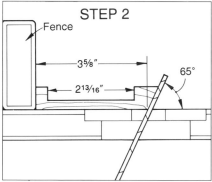

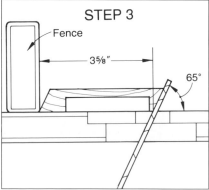

along the top, pointed edge of the back where shown on the Exploded View drawing *below.*

4. As shown at *right,* glue and clamp the grooved back piece to the base 1¼" from the base's front edge. To prevent denting the back piece, use a clamp with plastic

Plastic pad

pads on the heads or use softwood clamp blocks.

5. Finish-sand the holder and apply the finish.

Add the mechanism and feet

1. Cut the Velcro supplied with the calendar into four 3"-long pieces. Peel off the backing, and stick two of the Velcro pieces to the back of the calendar, being careful not to cover the battery cover. For better adhesion between the Velcro and wood, use steel wool to rub the dadoed area of the back piece. Adhere the two remaining pieces to the dadoed area where shown in the Exploded View drawing.

2. Finally, apply four self-sticking bumpers or felt pads (like those used on cabinet door backs) to the bottom of the base.

3. Using the instructions supplied with the calendar, set the functions, and position the calendar in the dadoed recess.

Buying Guide

•**Digital calendar.** Mechanism, battery, and 6" of Velcro for $24.95. New Products International, 15 West Street, Spring Valley, NY 10977. Sorry, no phone orders.

Project Tool List
Tablesaw
   Dado blade or dado set
Finishing sander

Note: *We built the project using the tools listed. You may be able to substitute other tools or equipment for listed items you don't have. Additional common hand tools and clamps may be required to complete the project.*

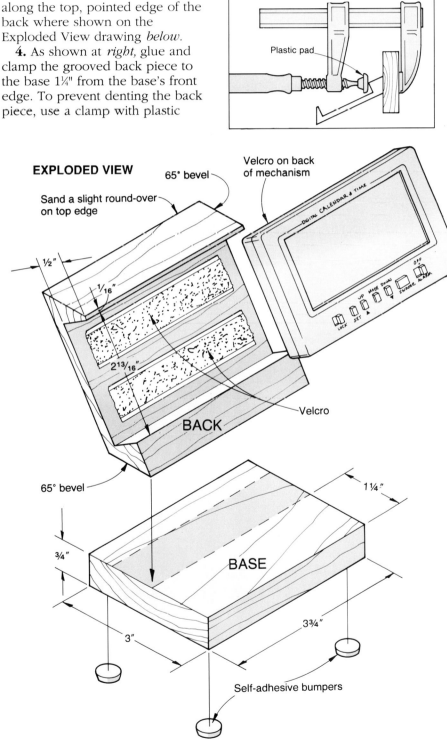

EXPLODED VIEW

65° bevel

Sand a slight round-over on top edge

Velcro on back of mechanism

½"

1/16"

2 13/16"

BACK

Velcro

65° bevel

¾"

3"

BASE

1¼"

3¾"

Self-adhesive bumpers

NEW HORIZON DESK SET

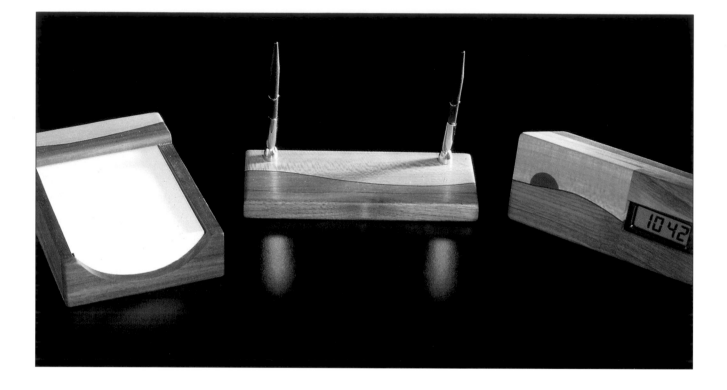

Who wouldn't be tickled to receive this finely crafted desk set from your workshop? The wavy "horizon" design places this gift at the head of its class. One lamination yields enough of the horizon pieces for two complete desk sets.

Laminating the horizon design

1. To make the lamination for the three desk items, start by cutting the maple (A) and walnut (B) to size as dimensioned in the Bill of Materials *opposite*, plus 1" in length.

2. Bore a 1" hole ⅜" deep in the maple for the sun where indicated on the Lamination Grid drawing,

opposite, top. Resaw a scrap of cardinal wood or padauk to ⁷⁄₁₆" thick and, using a 1" plug cutter, cut a plug for the sun (C). Glue the plug in the 1" hole. After the glue dries, sand the plug flush.

3. Sketch a curved horizon line across the maple as laid out in the Lamination Grid drawing, being sure to bisect the cardinal wood plug. (We give you the line patterns for our desk set, but don't be afraid to improvise. Any gently curved line will do.)

4. Temporarily attach the maple atop the walnut with a few small beads of hotmelt adhesive or double-faced tape. Joint the edges and trim the ends of the lamination

to ensure that both pieces are perfectly flush.

5. Using a bandsaw with a ⅜" or ¼" fine-toothed blade, cut the horizon line through the lamination.

6. Separate the maple from the walnut. (By matching each maple piece with its corresponding walnut piece, you'll end up with two horizon scenes, as shown in the Desk-Set Lamination drawing, *opposite, middle*.)

Note: *The rest of this project explains how to make one complete desk set from one of the horizon lamination scenes.*

7. Mark and cut the lower curved line through the walnut (see the

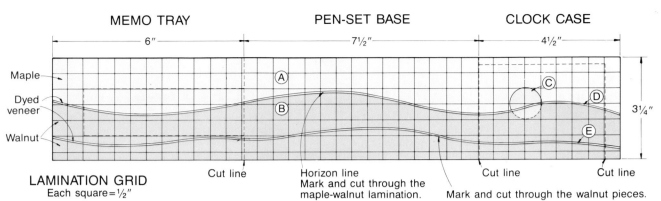

MEMO TRAY   PEN-SET BASE   CLOCK CASE

6"   7½"   4½"

Maple

Dyed veneer

Walnut

3¼"

LAMINATION GRID
Each square = ½"

Cut line

Horizon line
Mark and cut through the maple-walnut lamination.

Cut line   Cut line

Mark and cut through the walnut pieces.

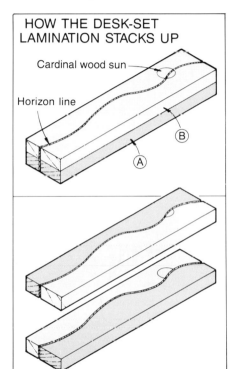

HOW THE DESK-SET LAMINATION STACKS UP

Cardinal wood sun

Horizon line

B

A

Bill of Materials					
Part	Finished Size*			Mat.	Qty.
	T	W	L		
BASIC LAMINATION					
A*	¾"	3¼"	18"	M	1
B*	¾"	3¼"	18"	W	1
C	⁷⁄₁₆"	1" diam.		C	1
D*	¹⁄₂₈"	¾"	18¼"	BV	1
E*	¹⁄₂₈"	¾"	18¼"	GV	1
MEMO TRAY					
F*	⅜"	1½"	5"	W	2
G*	⅜"	1½"	6¼"	W	2
H	¼"	4½"	6¼"	PLY	1
CLOCK CASE					
I*	¾"	3¼"	6¾"	W	2
J*	⅝"	1"	2¾"	W	2

*These parts are cut larger initially, then trimmed to finished size. Please read the instructions before cutting.

Material Key: M—maple, W—walnut, C—cardinal wood, BV—black veneer, GV—green veneer, PLY—plywood
Supplies: Hotmelt adhesive or double-faced tape.

Lamination Grid drawing for the line's location).

8. Rip and crosscut two strips of veneer (D, E) as dimensioned in the Bill of Materials. (We used dyed veneers, but you could substitute two thin strips [¹⁄₁₆" or less] of different-colored woods. We cut the veneer with a straightedge and sharp X-acto knife.)

9. Glue parts A, B, D, and E together as shown in photo A *below,* keeping the ends and surfaces of A and B flush.

10. After the glue has thoroughly dried, scrape off the excess glue and protruding veneer. Plane or resaw the lamination to ⅝" thick. Sand all surfaces smooth.

11. Lay out and mark the sections for the memo tray, pen-set base, and clock case as dimensioned in
continued

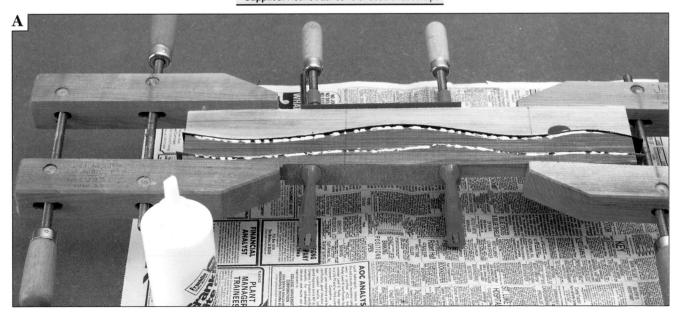

A

NEW HORIZON DESK SET

continued

the Lamination Grid drawing. Cut the three items to size.

Making the pen-set base

1. Mark the location of and bore two ½" holes ¼" deep in the bottom of the pen-set base. Drill a ⅛" hole through the center of the ½" hole and test-fit the pen funnels.

2. Remove the funnels and round-over the top edges by sanding. Sand the base smooth and apply an oil finish. Attach the funnels.

Building the memo tray

1. Rip and crosscut a piece of ½"- or ¾"-thick walnut to 1½" wide and 25" long. Resaw or plane the walnut stock to ⅜" thick. (We planed ours to size, removing about 1/32" with each pass. We used a push block when moving the stock over the rotating-jointer blades.)

2. Crosscut a 14" section from the 25"-long piece. Cut a ¼" dado ⅛" deep ⅛" from the bottom edge of the 14" piece. (We cut ours on a router table with a ¼" straight bit.) Crosscut the front and back of the tray (F) from the remaining 11" section, and the two sides (G) from the 14" section.

3. Mark and cut a 3" radius on the front piece. Cut the bottom (H) to size from plywood or thin stock.

4. Glue and clamp the tray together, checking for square.

5. Reduce the ⅝" thickness of the memo pad lamination to ⅜" using a bandsaw or hand plane. (Due to its short length, we clamped the lamination in our workbench end vise and used a hand plane to reduce its thickness. Stock shorter than 8" should *never* be planed on the jointer.)

6. Round-over the front edge of the lamination (you can either sand the edge or use a router table with a fence and a ¼" round-over bit).

7. Sand the laminate and the tray smooth. Glue and clamp the two subassemblies together. Later, remove the clamps, finish-sand, and apply an oil finish.

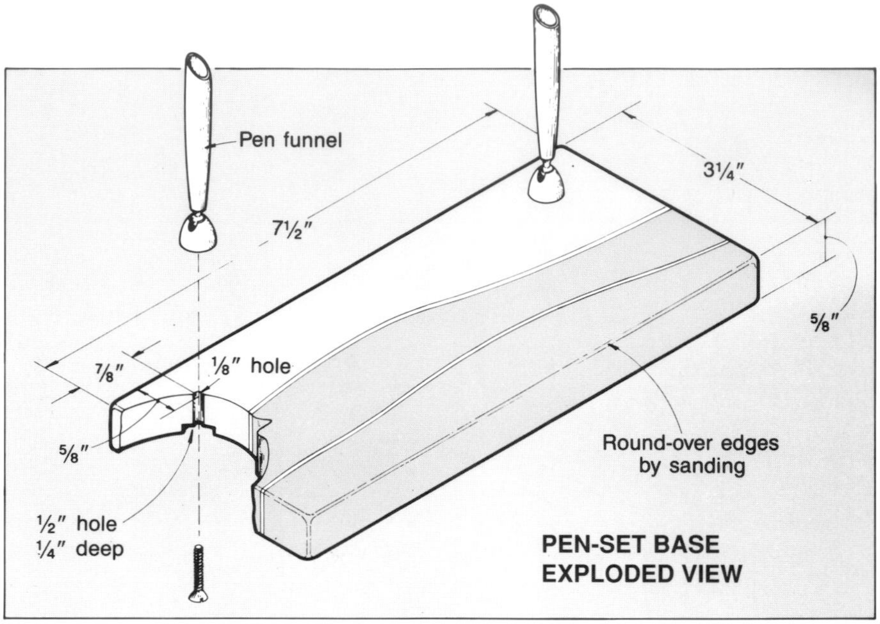
Pen funnel
3¼"
7½"
⅝"
⅞"
⅛" hole
⅝"
Round-over edges by sanding
½" hole
¼" deep
PEN-SET BASE
EXPLODED VIEW

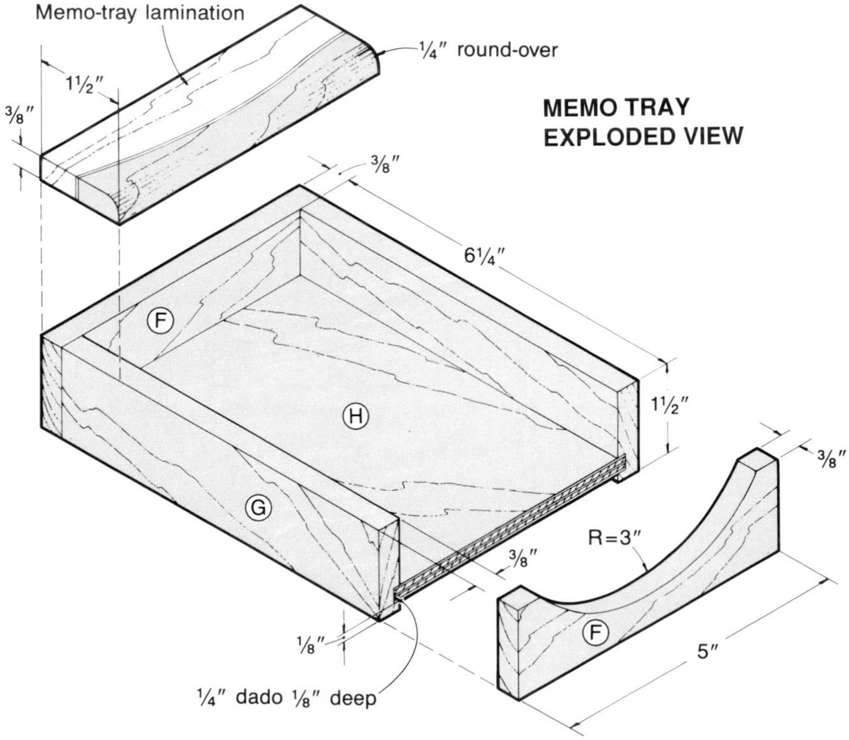
Memo-tray lamination
¼" round-over
1½"
⅜"
MEMO TRAY
EXPLODED VIEW
⅜"
6¼"
F
H
1½"
⅜"
G
R=3"
⅜"
⅛"
F
5"
¼" dado ⅛" deep

Constructing the clock case

1. Rip and crosscut the walnut parts (I) to size. Then, rip and crosscut a ¾" piece of walnut 1" wide by 12" long for the clock brackets (J). Resaw or plane this 12" piece to ⅝" thick. Cut a ½" rabbet ⅛" deep the length of the piece. Sand a slight round-over on the outside edge of the rabbet. Cut this rabbeted piece into two 2¾" lengths (J).

2. Glue and clamp the clock's parts together. Be sure to leave enough space for the digital clock. (We cut a scrap spacer the same size as the clock, inset it while clamping, and removed it before the glue dried.)

3. Remove the clamps and mark the 10°-angled ends of the clock body. Bevel both ends on the bandsaw as shown in photo B at *right*.

4. Set the table saw blade at 10° from vertical center. Bevel-rip both edges of the clock body as shown in photo C, *below right*.

5. Sand a slight round-over on the edges. Sand the clock body smooth and apply an oil finish.

Buying Guide

• **Liquid crystal (LCD) clock.** Stock #16011 without an alarm; #16002 with an alarm. For current prices, contact Klockit, P.O. Box 629, Lake Geneva, WI 53147, or call 800-556-2548 to order.

• **Pen and funnel.** Gold colored, super deluxe. Stock #42004. For current prices, contact Klockit (address above).

• **Color-dyed veneers**. Come in eight different colors in widths from 4" to 10" (minimum width of 4" for this project), 36" long, and 1/28" thick. Jet Black stock #DV131 and Tropic Green stock #DV123. For current prices, contact Constantine, 2050 Eastchester Rd., Bronx, NY 10461, or call 800-223-8087 to order.

Project Tool List

Tablesaw
Bandsaw
Jointer
Drill press
   Bits: 1/8", 1"
   1" plug cutter
Router
   Router table
   Bits: 1/4" straight, 1/4" round-over
Finishing sander

Note: *We built the project using the tools listed. You may be able to substitute other tools or equipment for listed items you don't have. Additional common hand tools and clamps may be required to complete the project.*

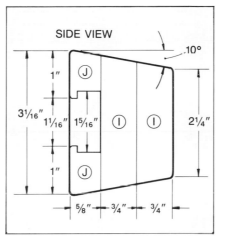

SIDE VIEW

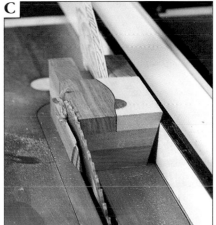

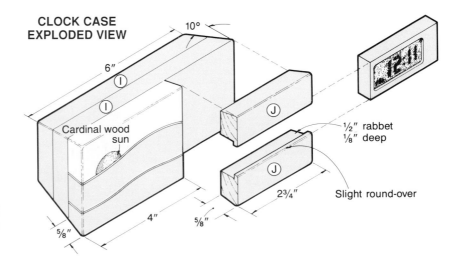

CLOCK CASE EXPLODED VIEW

Cardinal wood sun

1/2" rabbet 1/8" deep

Slight round-over

FORTUNE-FOUR DESK ACCESSORIES

Expect a handsome return on investment of your time when you incorporate two popular hardwoods into one high-yield design. A careful search of your (wood) stock portfolio could uncover all the resources you need to get started in this business adventure.

Start by assembling all of the laminations

1. To make up the lamination strips, rip and crosscut ten ½x⅝x12⅛" maple pieces and eight ½x⅛x12⅛" walnut pieces.

2. Lay out two laminations with five maple strips alternated with four of the narrow walnut strips in between as shown on the Cutting Diagram at *far right.* Glue and clamp each lamination, as shown

below. (We aligned the pieces at the ends, and clamped a bar across each lamination end to keep all pieces flat while the glue cured.)

3. Assemble the third, smaller lamination using the three ⅞₆x½x8½" maple pieces and two ³⁄₃₂x½x8½" walnut pieces. Now, glue and clamp them, alternating the narrow walnut strips between the maple.

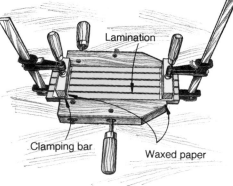

Lamination

Clamping bar

Waxed paper

After the glue dries, remove the clamps, scrape off the glue squeeze-out from one face, and resaw or plane the piece to ³⁄₁₆" thick. (We used a feather board and pushstick to safely saw this lamination and the other small pieces on our tablesaw.)

4. Remove the clamps from the two large laminations, and scrape off glue squeeze-out. Next, sand both sides on the laminations, starting with 150-grit sandpaper and ending with 220-grit paper. Now, finish-sand both laminations to ⅞₆" final thickness.

5. Make copies of the full-sized patterns *opposite.* (We used carbon paper.) Mark all hole centerpoints on the patterns. Now, separate the patterns. (We used one pattern for parts A and B.)

Let's make the pad and pen holder next

1. With a pencil, transfer the pattern outlines of parts A and B and the hole centerpoint onto the face of one lamination. (We turned the pattern over to trace part A. See the lamination Cutting Diagram *below* for how we laid out the parts on the three laminations.) For a left-handed person, consider

continued

Cutting Diagram

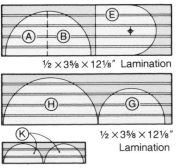

½ × 3⅝ × 12⅛" Lamination

½ × 3⅝ × 12⅛" Lamination

³⁄₁₆ × 1⁹⁄₁₆ × 8½" Lamination

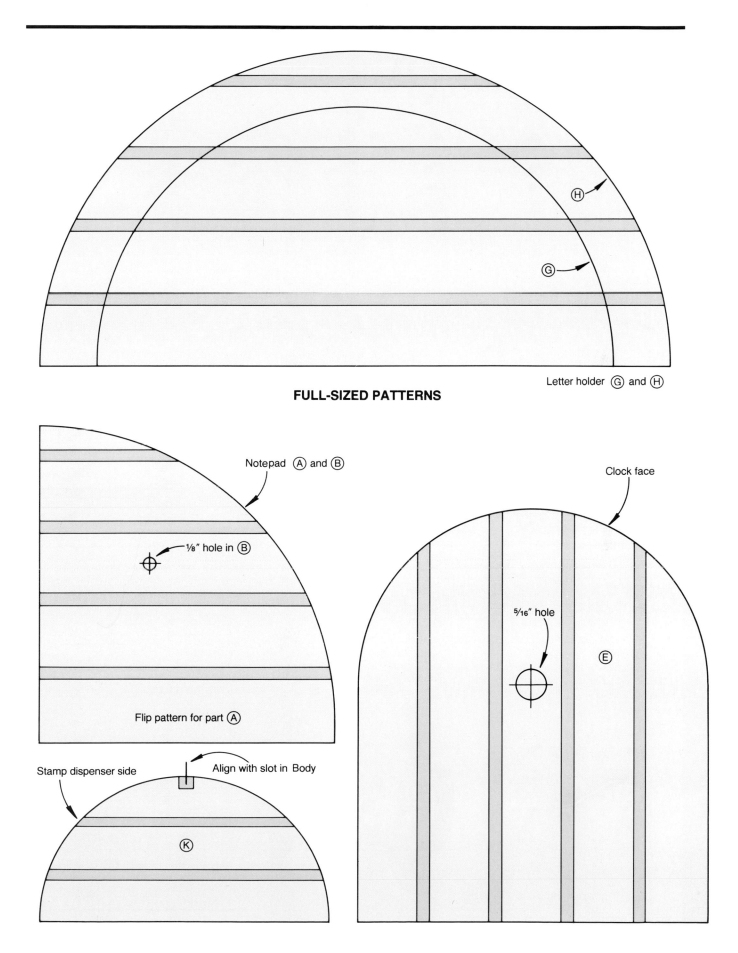

FULL-SIZED PATTERNS

Letter holder Ⓖ and Ⓗ

Notepad Ⓐ and Ⓑ

⅛″ hole in Ⓑ

Flip pattern for part Ⓐ

Clock face

5/16″ hole

Ⓔ

Stamp dispenser side

Align with slot in Body

Ⓚ

FORTUNE-FOUR DESK ACCESSORIES

continued

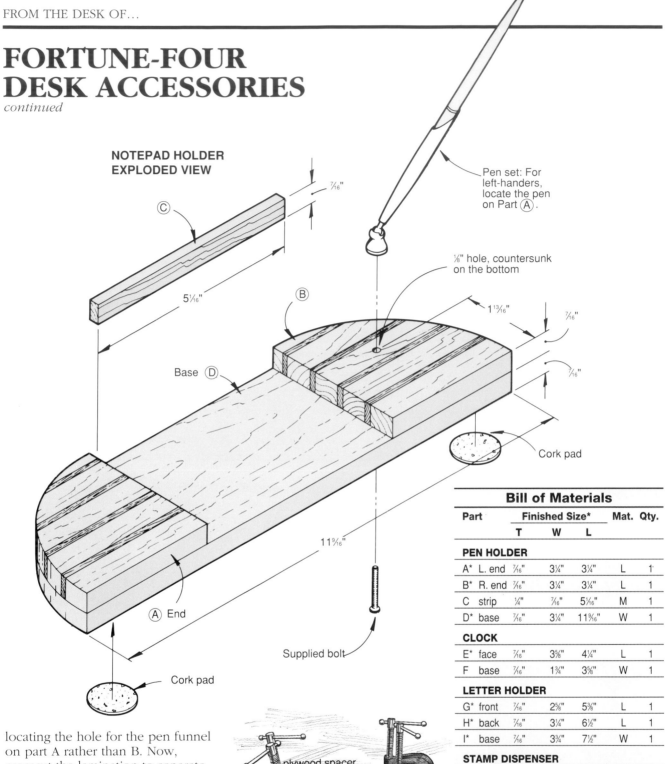

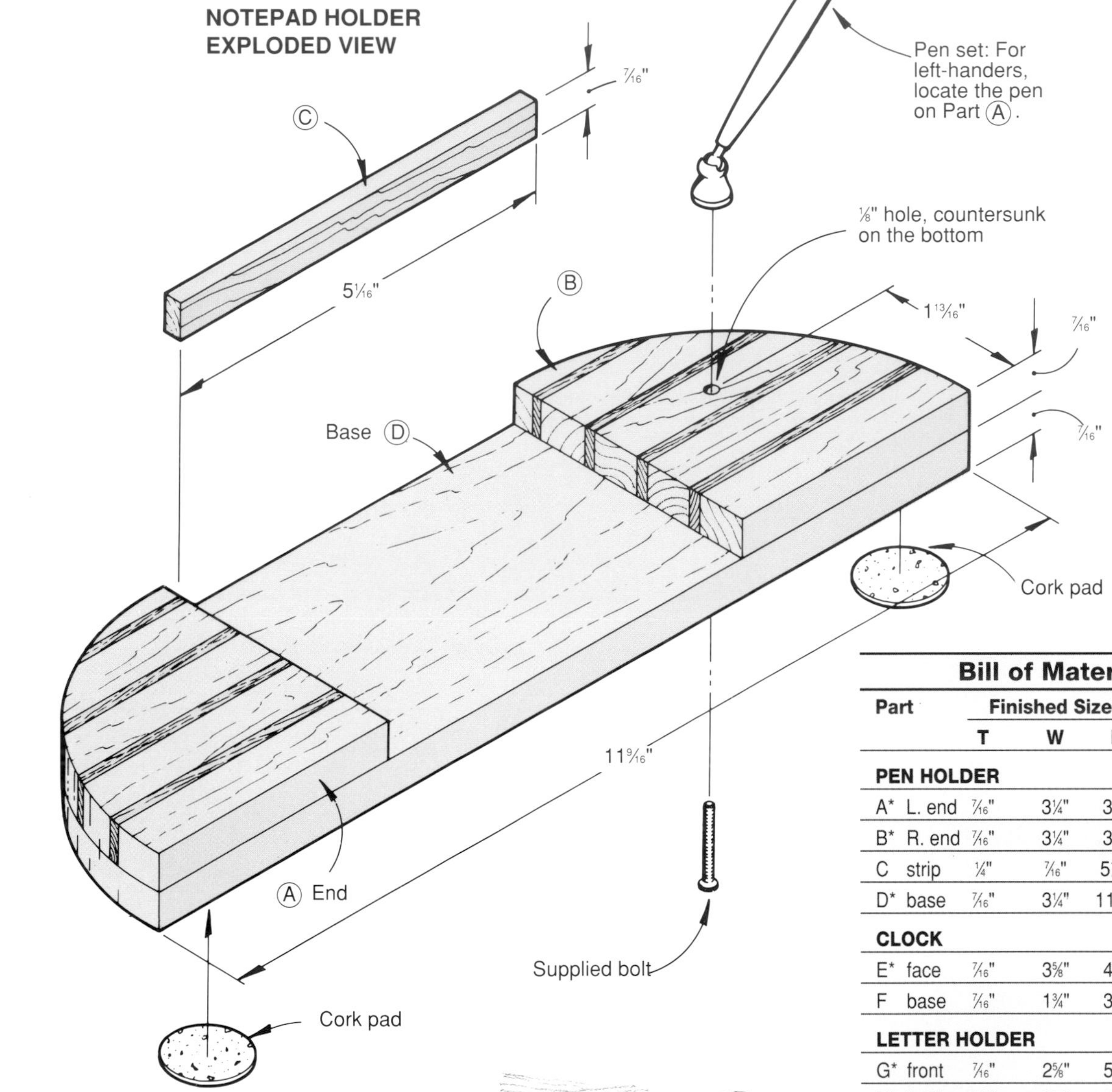
NOTEPAD HOLDER
EXPLODED VIEW
7/16"
C
5 1/16"
B
Base D
Pen set: For left-handers, locate the pen on Part A.
1/8" hole, countersunk on the bottom
1 13/16"
7/16"
7/16"
Cork pad
11 9/16"
A End
Supplied bolt
Cork pad

locating the hole for the pen funnel on part A rather than B. Now, crosscut the lamination to separate parts A and B, but *do not* bandsaw the curved edges yet.

2. For part C, rip and crosscut one maple strip to 1/4X7/16X5 1/16", and for the base (D), one walnut piece to 7/16 3 1/4X11 3/4". From 1/4" plywood, cut a spacer 1/16" wider and longer than your notepad. (We designed our holder for 3X5" self-stick notepads.)

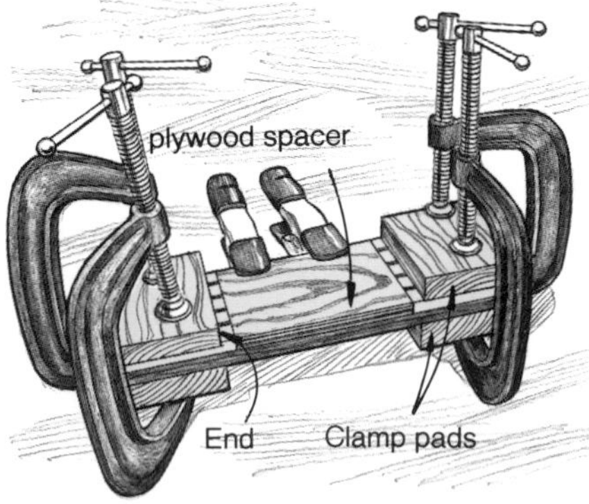
plywood spacer
End
Clamp pads

Bill of Materials

Part	Finished Size* T	W	L	Mat.	Qty.
PEN HOLDER					
A* L. end	7/16"	3 1/4"	3 1/4"	L	1
B* R. end	7/16"	3 1/4"	3 1/4"	L	1
C strip	1/4"	7/16"	5 1/16"	M	1
D* base	7/16"	3 1/4"	11 9/16"	W	1
CLOCK					
E* face	7/16"	3 5/8"	4 1/4"	L	1
F base	7/16"	1 3/4"	3 5/8"	W	1
LETTER HOLDER					
G* front	7/16"	2 5/8"	5 3/8"	L	1
H* back	7/16"	3 1/4"	6 1/2"	L	1
I* base	7/16"	3 3/4"	7 1/2"	W	1
STAMP DISPENSER					
J* body	1 1/16"	1 1/2"	3"	W	1
K* sides	3/16"	1 1/2"	3"	L	2
L base	3/8"	1 5/8"	3 1/4"	W	1

*Cut parts marked with an * to final size during construction. Please read the instructions before cutting.

Material Key: L—lamination, M—maple, W—walnut.
Supplies: #6X3/4" and #6X1" flathead wood screws

3. Dry-assemble the holder parts as shown on the Notepad Holder drawing *opposite*. Align the edges of parts A and B with the front edge of the base. Next, apply double-faced tape to the back of the spacer and position it between A and B. Place part C behind the spacer. Clamp all parts in place. Now, glue parts A, B, and C to the base, and clamp as shown *opposite, bottom*. Wipe off glue squeeze-out with a damp cloth.

4. Remove the clamps and drill the ⅛" hole for the pen's bolt. (See the Buying Guide on *page 49* for our hardware source.) Now, bandsaw and sand the round corners of A, B, and D. (We sawed slightly wide of the line, and then sanded to the curved lines with our disc sander.) Now, finish-sand the holder. See Step 5 on *page 49* for finishing information.

It's time to move on to the clock

1. Trace the Clock Face (E) pattern outline onto the back side of the laminate piece left from parts A and B. (We ran the lamination vertically.) Mark the hole center-point on the back.

2. Center a 3" Forstner bit on the centerpoint, and bore a ⅛"-deep hole into the back. Or, make a template and rout the recess with a straight bit. On the same centerpoint, drill a ⁵⁄₁₆"-diameter hole through the part. (When drilling, we backed the piece with scrap to prevent chip-out.) Now, bandsaw the top to shape, and sand the edge using techniques described earlier.

3. From walnut, rip and crosscut a piece to ⁷⁄₁₆x1¾x5" for the clock base (F). Mount a ⁷⁄₁₆" dado on your tablesaw, angle it 5° from perpendicular, and make a test-cut in scrap to test the fit of the face in the dado. Adjust width if necessary. Next, starting ½" in from the front edge, cut the ¼"-deep groove lengthwise in the piece. See the Clock Exploded View and Side View drawings *above* and *right* for additional details. Now, cut the base to final length, finish-sand both parts, and shape the base edges.

4. Glue the clock face in the base groove. After the glue has cured, assemble the clock as shown on the Clock Exploded View drawing. Shorten the hands. (We cut ¼" from each.) Remove the movement and finish.

Try this simple and effective letter holder

1. Transfer the letter-holder front (G) and back (H) patterns to the face of the second lamination. Bandsaw or scrollsaw the curved parts to shape, and sand the cut edges.

2. To form the base (I), rip and crosscut a piece of walnut to ⁷⁄₁₆x4x8". Find the centerpoint along one edge of the piece and using a compass, scribe a 3¾" radius on the bottom of the base. Next, using the dimensions on the Letter Holder
continued

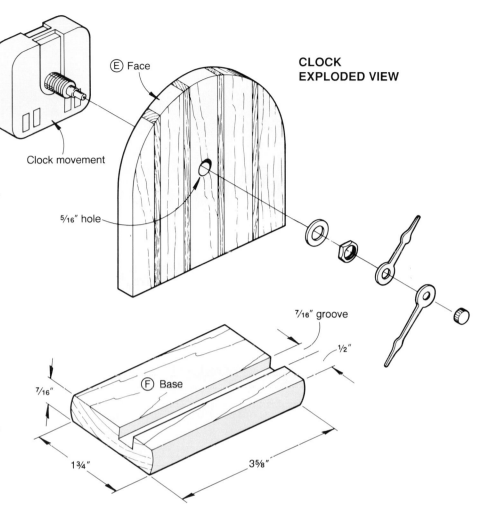

E Face

Clock movement

CLOCK EXPLODED VIEW

⁵⁄₁₆" hole

⁷⁄₁₆" groove

½"

⁷⁄₁₆"

F Base

1¾"

3⅝"

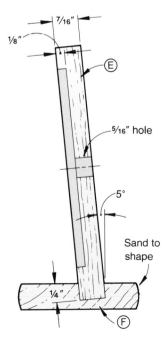

SIDE VIEW

⁷⁄₁₆"

⅛"

E

⁵⁄₁₆" hole

5°

Sand to shape

¼"

F

FORTUNE-FOUR DESK ACCESSORIES

continued

drawing at *right,* locate the centerpoints of the four screw holes. Drill %₄" shank holes where marked and countersink them on the bottom face. Now, bandsaw or scrollsaw the base to shape. Finish-sand the piece.

3. To assemble the letter holder, first apply glue to the bottom of the back (H) and position it on the base. (We ripped a strip of ⅛₆"-thick scrap to space the back on the base, and used a marking gauge to center it ½" from each end.) Let the glue set for five minutes. Now, turn the assembly upside down and place its back in a vise. Using the existing holes, drill ³⁄₃₂" pilot holes ⅝" deep into the back. Drive a #6×1" flathead wood screw into each hole.

4. From scrap, cut a 1½"-wide spacer 4" long and place it against the back. Apply glue to the bottom edge of the front piece, place it against the spacer, and center. After the glue sets, drill the pilot holes and drive the screws. Apply finish.

Top off your set with our nifty stamp dispenser

1. Rip and crosscut a walnut piece to 1¹⁄₁₆×1¹⁄₁₆×4" for the stamp-box body (J). Scribe a vertical centerline on one face of the piece and mark a centerpoint ¹¹⁄₁₆" up from the bottom edge as shown on the Stamp Dispenser and Body Detail drawings *opposite.* From that centerpoint, mark a ¾" radius, and scribe a line from each edge of the radius to the bottom. Remove the U-shaped section. (We first bored a 1½"-diameter hole through the piece, and then bandsawed along the vertical lines.) Now, saw the body piece in two as shown at *right.*

2. Crosscut the thin lamination in half. Next, glue and clamp the two body pieces to the face of one of the side pieces (K). Glue and clamp the second side to the walnut body.

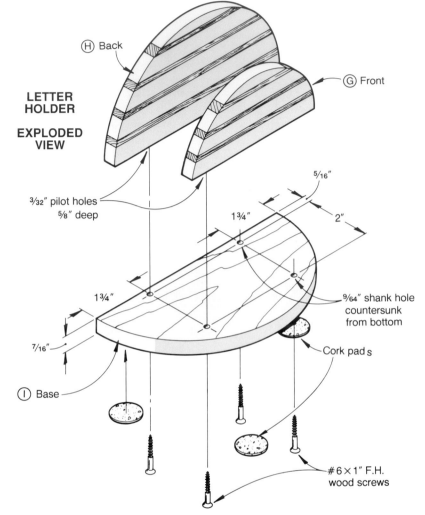

LETTER HOLDER

EXPLODED VIEW

(H) Back

(G) Front

³⁄₃₂" pilot holes ⅝" deep

5/16"

1¾"

2"

1¾"

9/64" shank hole countersunk from bottom

Cork pad s

7/16"

(I) Base

#6 × 1" F.H. wood screws

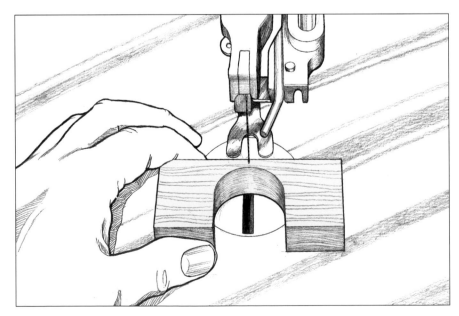

3. Transfer the Stamp Dispenser Side pattern to one side of the assembly. Saw the dispenser to shape. Finish-sand the assembly.

4. For the base (L), rip and crosscut a piece of ⅜"-thick walnut to 1⅝×3¼". Mark, drill, and countersink the 5/32" shank hole where dimensioned. Finish-sand the base. Now, center the dispenser on the base and mark the pilot hole. Drill the 3/32" pilot hole ½" deep.

5. Apply the finish of your choice. (We applied one coat of sanding sealer and two coats of lacquer.)

6. Adhere ½"-diameter cork pads to the base of the letter holder and the notepad holder.

7. Attach the pen funnel to the notepad holder, and then screw the base to the stamp dispenser. Mount the clock works, attach the hands, insert a battery, and set the time.

Buying Guide
•**Desk kit.** Includes black-matte pen, gold funnel, quartz clock movement, hands, and self-adhesive cork pads. For current prices, contact Schlabaugh & Sons, P.O. Box 327, Kalona, IA 52247, or call 800-346-9663 or 319-656-2374.

Project Tool List
Tablesaw
Dado blade or dado set
Bandsaw or scrollsaw
Drill press
Bits: 3/32", ⅛", 9/64", 5/32", 5/16", 1½", 3"
Finishing sander

Note: We built the project using the tools listed. You may be able to substitute other tools or equipment for listed items you don't have. Additional common hand tools and clamps may be required to complete the project.

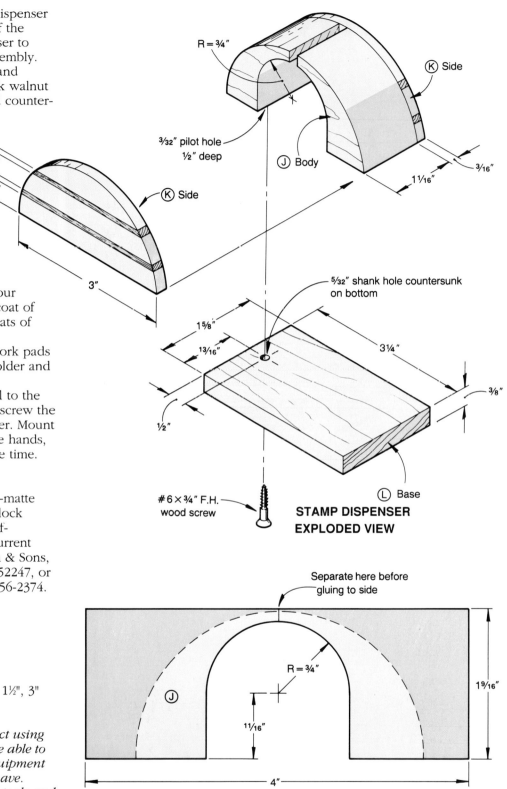

R = ¾"

Ⓚ Side

3/32" pilot hole
½" deep

Ⓙ Body

1 1/16"

3/16"

3/32"

7/16"

3/32"   7/16"

Ⓚ Side

3"

5/32" shank hole countersunk on bottom

1⅝"

13/16"

3¼"

3/8"

½"

#6 × ¾" F.H. wood screw

Ⓛ Base

STAMP DISPENSER EXPLODED VIEW

Separate here before gluing to side

R = ¾"

Ⓙ

11/16"

1 9/16"

4"

BODY DETAIL

EXECUTIVE NAMEPLATE

F irst impressions mean a lot, particularly in the business world. At your workplace, you want to project yourself as a well-established professional. The way you dress, speak, and behave go a long way toward this end. But so do the things around you—including the nameplate on your desk. Our oak and walnut rendition lets you introduce yourself with dignity, and a touch of class. Best of all, you can knock it out in a few hours.

Let's start with the oak plate

1. Determine the length of the oak plate (A) you'll need by arranging the letters of the name on the sticky side of a strip of masking tape as shown at *right*. Measure the length of the name. Then, add 1⅛" for a margin at each end. (We used ¾"-high laser-cut walnut letters and spaced them between ⅟₁₆" and ⅛" apart. See the Buying Guide *opposite.*)

2. To make the oak plate (A), plane or resaw a thicker piece to ¼" thick, or use ¼"-thick oak plywood. Rip the piece to 1½" wide and crosscut it to the length you determined in step 1.

Form the walnut trim

1. To shape the walnut trim pieces (B, C), rip a strip of walnut to ½" square. You'll need a length equal to twice the nameplate's length and twice the nameplate's width, with a few extra inches to cover mitering waste.

2. Mount a ¼" core-box bit in a table-mounted router, and raise the

bit ⅛" above the table surface. Make an auxiliary fence from scrap, position it against the fence so the front edge centers on the bit as shown on the drawing *below.* Clamp the fence in place. Now, holding the auxiliary fence against the table fence and above the bit, turn on the router and slowly lower the auxiliary fence onto the bit. Move it slightly to enlarge the routed area around the bit. Turn off the router. Place double-faced tape on the back of the auxiliary fence and stick it to the table fence. Now, rout a cove along one edge of the ½"-square strip.

3. To bevel the strip, set the rip fence on your table saw ⁵⁄₁₆" from the blade. Angle the blade to 30° from center as shown *opposite, top.* Rip the bevel. (Note in the drawing that we clamped feather boards at the side and top to hold the strip firmly against the fence. We used a long stick of the same size as the strip for a push rod.) Sand the molding smooth.

4. Lay the oak plate along the coved edge of the molded walnut strip and mark the length of each side on the strip's edge. (Leave enough space between each set of marks to allow for mitering waste.) Extend 45° cutoff lines outward from these marks on the flat back surface of the strip. Mitercut all four

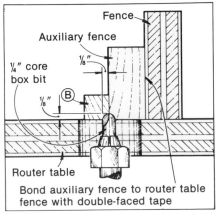

Fence

Auxiliary fence

¼" core box bit

⅛"

B

⅛"

Router table

Bond auxiliary fence to router table fence with double-faced tape

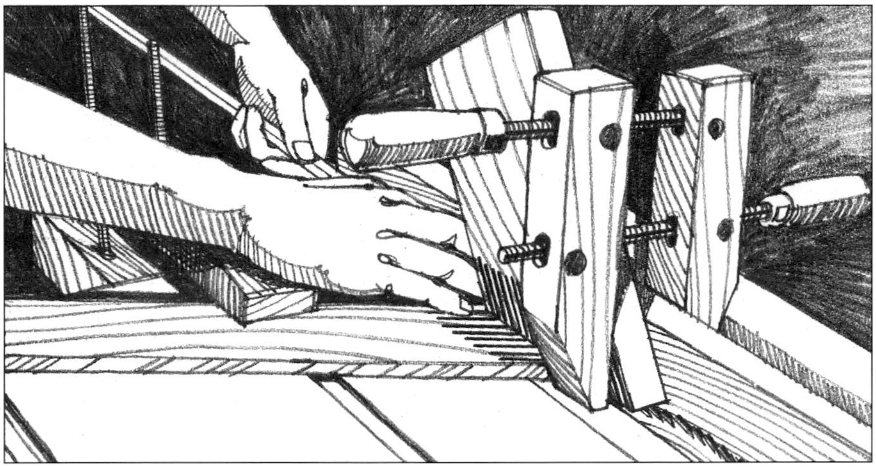

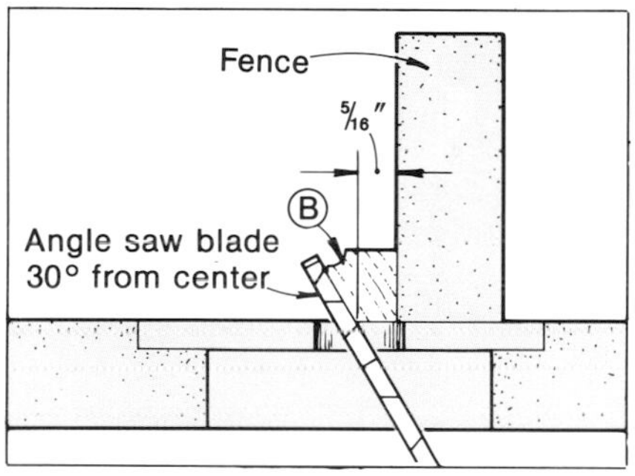

trim pieces (B, C) to length. Test-fit the pieces.

Now, the final assembly

1. To apply the letters, clamp a straightedge onto the oak plate, 7/16" from the top edge. Pencil faint vertical lines 1⅝" in from the edges to mark the margins for the first and last letters. Arrange the letters on the plate until you are satisfied with the spacing. Make a faint pencil mark on the plate along the left side of each letter. Apply glue to the back of each letter. Position the top of the letter against the straightedge and the left edge on the pencil line.

2. Place the oak plate on a sheet of waxed paper. Apply a bead of glue to all edges of the oak plate, assemble the molding strips around it, and clamp. Remove glue squeeze-out with a damp cloth. After the glue dries, remove clamps and sand excess glue.

3. To make the nameplate supports (D), trace the pattern found on the Full-Sized Support pattern and Section View, *below left,* onto a piece of ⅜"-thick walnut. Cut the parts to shape. Sand the supports smooth and glue them to the back of the nameplate two inches in from the ends where shown on the Exploded View drawing *below.*

4. Now, finish the nameplate. (We sprayed on two coats of clear lacquer.)

Buying Guide

- **Walnut letters.** ¾" tall. For current prices, contact Paddle Tramps Mfg. Co., 1317 University Ave., Lubbock, TX 79401, or call 806-765-9901.

Project Tool List

Tablesaw
Scrollsaw or bandsaw
Router
  Router table
  ¼" core box bit
Finishing sander

Note: *We built the project using the tools listed. You may be able to substitute other tools or equipment for listed items you don't have. Additional common hand tools and clamps may be required to complete the project.*

Bill of Materials

Part	T	W	L	Mat.	Qty.
A plate	¼"	1½"	variable	O	1
B* trim	½"	½"	variable	W	2
C* trim	½"	½"	2½"	W	2
D* supports	⅜"	1¼"	2¼"	W	2

(T, W, L = Finished Size*)

*Cut parts marked with an * larger initally, and then trim to finished size. Please read the instructions before cutting.

Material Key: O—oak, W—walnut
Supplies: waxed paper, masking tape, finish.

FULL-SIZED SUPPORT PATTERN and SECTION VIEW

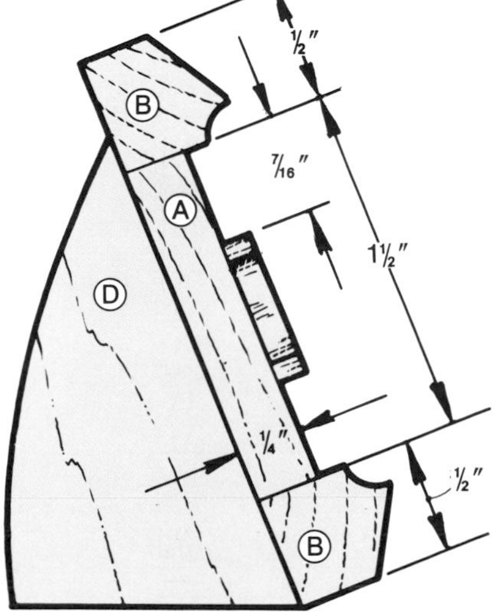

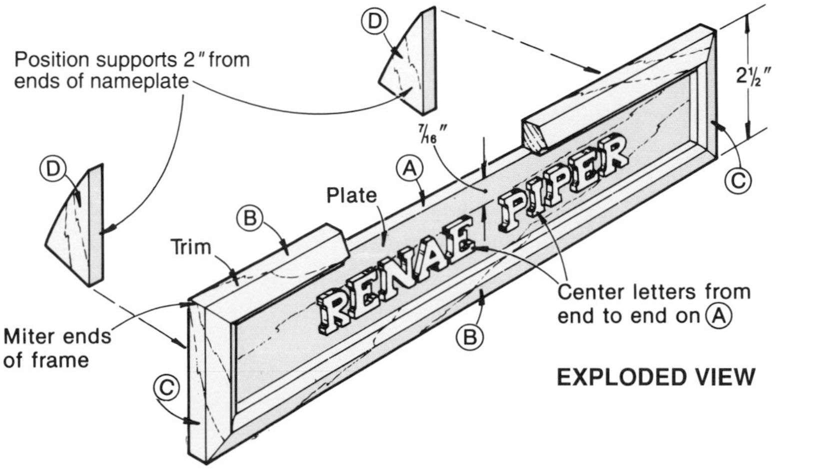

EXPLODED VIEW

WHALE STAMP BOX

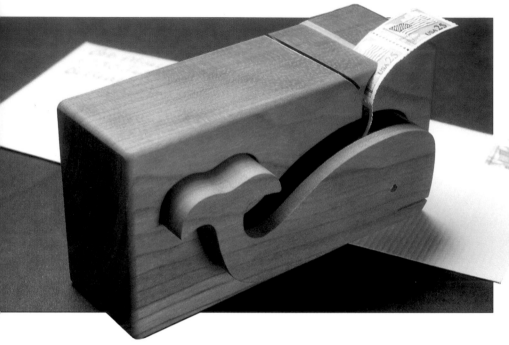

Sail the seven seas and you won't find a better looking stamp box than our design *above.* Cut on a bandsaw, it features a whale-shaped drawer that slides out with the push of a finger for stamp refilling. One of the two saw kerfs making the whale's spout lets you dispense stamps quickly and easily.

Prepare the stock and pattern

1. Rip and crosscut a piece of hardwood to 1¾×3×5½". (We used cherry.) As shown on the Exploded View drawing at *right,* cut the whale-shaped drawer and surrounding block from this piece.

2. Transfer the full-sized whale pattern, *opposite top,* to the block. (We used carbon paper.) Mark the eye, mouth, spout lines, and the solid cutlines. Do not trace the dashed line, or the arrow lines at this time.

Cut out the whale

1. Using a bandsaw, cut the whale to shape. (We found a ⅛" blade with 12–14 teeth per inch

worked well.) When sawing the pattern, follow the cutting sequence shown by the arrows on the pattern. Note in illustration A *opposite* that in making the first saw cut, you enter and exit the wood in straight lines.

2. Start the second saw cut at the exposed tip of the tail. Following the arrows on the pattern, saw around the tail. When you reach the other tail tip, stop. Now, back the saw out of the cut.

3. Make the third saw cut, again following the arrow on the pattern. When finished sawing, you will have cut three separate pieces.

Now, form the drawer

1. First make a safety jig. (We placed the whale cutout on a scrap of 2×4, outlined its shape with a pencil, and then cut out the whale-shaped cavity with a bandsaw.)

2. Place the whale cutout in the jig's cavity, and position both against the saw's fence. Next, adjust the fence to slice ¼" from the side of the whale. Make the cut as shown in illustration B. (We stuck a strip of duct tape to the side of the whale to help safely remove the thin piece after it was cut by the saw.) Readjust the fence, face the whale and jig in the opposite direction, and saw the second slice. You now have two ¼"-thick whale-shaped sides and the remaining whale-shaped block.

3. Next, using the pattern and carbon paper, trace the drawer outline (indicated by the dashed line on the full-sized pattern) onto the whale-shaped block. Bandsaw along the dashed line as shown in illustration C.

4. Sand the inside faces of the two ¼" whale slices, and the outside of the whale-shaped drawer. (We tacked sandpaper to a flat surface, and slowly rubbed the whale parts over the paper.)

5. Apply glue, assemble, and clamp the whale drawer

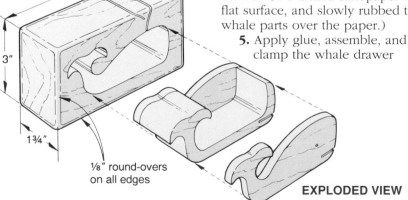

5½"

3"

1¾"

⅛" round-overs on all edges

EXPLODED VIEW

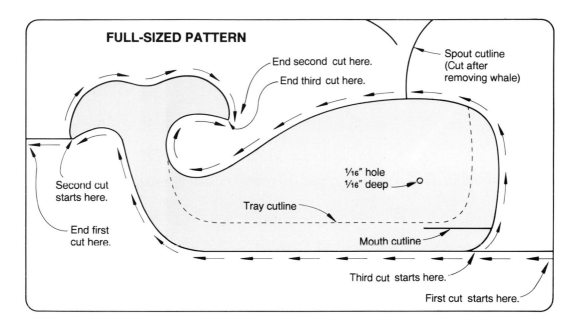

FULL-SIZED PATTERN

End second cut here.

End third cut here.

Spout cutline
(Cut after
removing whale)

Second cut
starts here.

End first
cut here.

¹⁄₁₆" hole
¹⁄₁₆" deep

Tray cutline

Mouth cutline

Third cut starts here.

First cut starts here.

pieces, checking alignment. After the glue has dried, remove the clamps. Next, using a bandsaw or scrollsaw, cut the mouth slit. Finally, drill the ¹⁄₁₆" holes for the eyes. (Avoid drilling through the sides). If needed, sand the edges just enough to remove roughsaw kerfs or burnt wood.

Assemble the block and apply the finish

1. Sand the inside surfaces of the top and bottom parts if needed to remove burnt wood. Next, apply glue to the mating surfaces, align the two parts, and then clamp them together. Remove the clamps after the glue has dried.

2. Set the fence on your tablesaw the same width as the assembled drawer. Raise the blade to the height of the block. Now, saw the excess width from the backside of the block. Finally, return to the bandsaw and make the two spout cuts where indicated. If the through-slit wants to close, wedge a piece of a flat toothpick in the slit on one edge to hold it open.

3. Sand a round-over on all outside edges of the block. Now, finish-sand all surfaces.

4. Apply the finish of your choice. (We sprayed on three coats of clear flat lacquer, sanding lightly between coats to level the surface.)

5. Insert the drawer in the block, place a roll of stamps in the drawer, and thread them through the spout.

Project Tool List
Tablesaw
Bandsaw
Portable drill
  ¹⁄₁₆" bit
Finishing sander

Note: *We built the project using the tools listed. You may be able to substitute other tools or equipment for listed items you don't have. Additional common hand tools and clamps may be required to complete the project.*

A

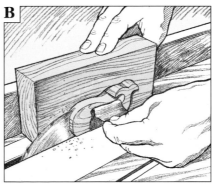

B

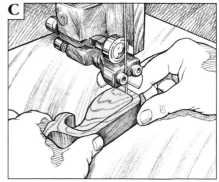

C

WRITE STUFF
HARDWOOD PENS

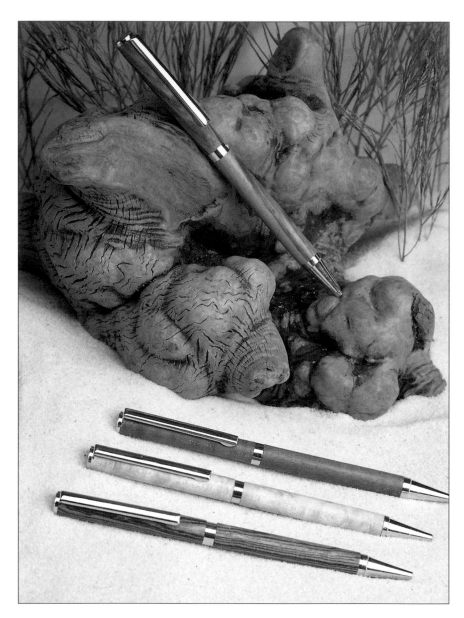

You don't have to own or operate a lathe—though that's an option—to turn beautiful pen barrels out of your favorite wood. We challenged Kim Downing, one of our talented draftsmen, to design an arbor assembly so our nonturning readers could make these pens on a drill press.

However you decide to make them, you can purchase the parts for five pens for about $15. Just add wood.

Preparing the pen barrels

1. Cut two pieces of stock to ⅝" square by 2⅛" long for the barrel blanks. Draw diagonals to find the center on one end of each blank.

2. Chuck a 7mm or ¾₂" bit into your drill press. (Although a ¾₂" bit will work, you'll get a better fit with a 7mm hole. See the Buying Guide *opposite* for our source.) Secure the barrel blank in a handscrew clamp, and check that the blank and bit are square with the drill-press table. Drill a 7mm hole through the length of the blank. Repeat with the other piece of stock.

3. With 150-grit sandpaper, rough up the outside surface of two pieces of the brass tube (see the Buying Guide for our source) for better adhesion in the next step.

4. Using gap-filling cyanoacrylate (instant) glue or 5-minute epoxy, coat the walls of the hole in each barrel blank. Push the brass tube into the stock, rotating the tube to distribute the adhesive. Repeat for the other barrel blank. If you get any adhesive in the brass tubes, let it cure, and then use the all-thread rod from the arbor assembly as a file to remove it.

5. Sand a ¾₆" chamfer along each corner of each blank (see End View detail *opposite, top,* for reference.)

Note: *To turn the pen barrels to shape on a lathe, you'll need to use the mandrel listed in the Buying*

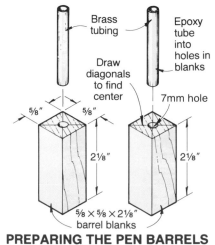

PREPARING THE PEN BARRELS

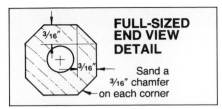

FULL-SIZED END VIEW DETAIL

Sand a 3/16" chamfer on each corner

3/16"
3/16"

Guide and shown in the drawing below right. To shape the pieces on the drill press, use the following instructions.

Build the arbor, and sand the barrels

1. Cut a piece of ¼"-diameter all-thread rod to 6¼" long. Fasten a barrel blank between the guide bushings and nuts where shown on the Arbor Setup drawing *below*. Tighten the nuts to secure the barrel blank to the all-thread rod.

2. Cut a piece of ½"- or ¾"-thick stock 2" wide and the length of your drill-press table for the guide block. Drill a ¼" hole in the middle of the guide block.

3. Place the guide block on the drill-press table. Place one end of the arbor assembly in the ¼" hole in the guide block, and fasten the opposite end in the drill-press chuck where shown in the Arbor Setup drawing. Clamp the guide block to the table.

4. With a rasp, coarse file, or 60-grit sandpaper wrapped around a piece of wood 2" wide, round the barrel to a diameter *just slightly larger than the bushings* as shown in the photo *below*. (We used a speed of about 1450 rpm.) *Be careful not to reduce the thickness of the guide bushings.* Using progressively finer grits of sandpaper, finish-sand the pen barrel flush with the outside surface of the bushings. Stop the drill press and do the final sanding with the grain. Repeat the procedure for the other pen barrel.

With the drill on, hand-sand the pen barrel blank flush with the outside surface of the guide bushings.

PEN ASSEMBLY

Clip
Barrel
Ring
Refill
Mechanism
Barrel
Tip

5. Add the finish to each barrel. Assemble the pieces as shown on the Pen Assembly drawing.

Buying Guide
• **Pen kit.** Two guide bushings plus enough parts (not including wood) for five pens, catalog no. IB500. For current prices, contact Craft Supplies, 1287 E. 1120 S., Provo, UT 84606, or call 800-551-8876 or 801-373-0917 to order.
• **Pen-turning mandrel and bit.** Mandrel with a #2 Morse taper, 7mm brad-point drill bit, and set of turning instructions, catalog no. GM050. For current prices, contact Craft Supplies, address above.

Project Tool List
Tablesaw
Drill press
 Bits: ¼", ⁹⁄₃₂"

Note: We built the project using the tools listed. You may be able to substitute other tools or equipment for listed items you don't have. Additional common hand tools and clamps may be required to complete the project.

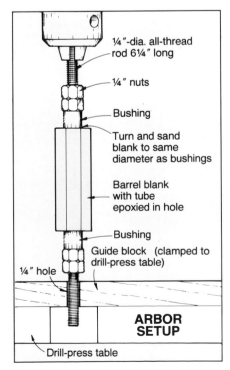

¼"-dia. all-thread rod 6¼" long

¼" nuts

Bushing

Turn and sand blank to same diameter as bushings

Bushing

Barrel blank with tube epoxied in hole

Bushing

Guide block (clamped to drill-press table)

¼" hole

ARBOR SETUP

Drill-press table

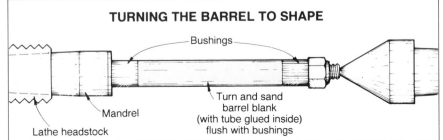

TURNING THE BARREL TO SHAPE

Bushings

Mandrel

Lathe headstock

Turn and sand barrel blank (with tube glued inside) flush with bushings

NOTEWORTHY NOTEPAD HOLDERS

lamination as shown on the drawing *below*. Raise the table saw blade about ¾" above the surface of the saw table, and tilt the blade 10° from center as shown in photo A *below*. Position the fence to align the blade with the angled cut line you just marked on the lamination and make the first cut as shown in the photo. Without moving the fence, make two more cuts, raising the blade about ¾" each pass.

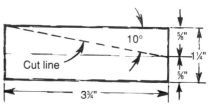

5. Without changing the blade angle, lower the blade below the surface of the saw table, and move the fence to the other side of the blade. (We moved the auxiliary wood fence to the other side of the rip fence at this point.) Raise the blade, reposition the fence, and

Ripping the walnut lamination with the saw blade set at 10° from center

S taying organized these days isn't easy. But having this quick-to-build project at the ready will help. We designed it to accept two sizes of Scotch Post-it Note Pads. Now, get ready for lots of requests for this one!

1. Rip and crosscut a piece of ¾" walnut to 4" wide by 22" long. (You need a piece this long for safety. It provides enough material for two holders.) Resaw or plane the piece to a ⅝" thickness.

2. Crosscut the 22"-long piece in half. Glue and clamp the two 11" pieces together face-to-face to form a 1¼"- thick lamination.

3. After the glue has dried, scrape the excess from one edge (not an end). Position the scraped edge against the table saw fence, and rip the opposite edge for a 3⅞" width. Then, rip the opposite edge for a 3¾" finished width.

4. Crosscut one end of the lamination. Mark an angled-cut line on the squared end of the

EXPLODED VIEW

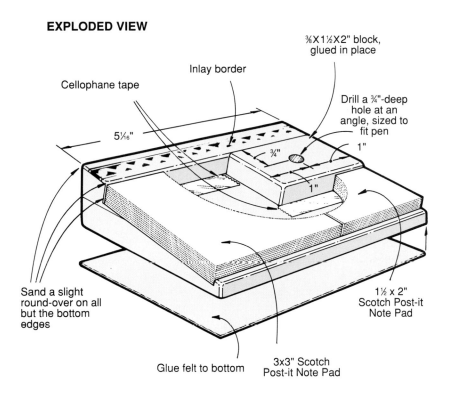

Cellophane tape

Inlay border

⅜X1½X2" block,
glued in place

Drill a ¾"-deep
hole at an
angle, sized to
fit pen

5¹⁄₁₆"

¾"

1"

1"

Sand a slight
round-over on all
but the bottom
edges

1½ x 2"
Scotch Post-it
Note Pad

Glue felt to bottom

3x3" Scotch
Post-it Note Pad

make two more cuts as shown in photo B *below* to finish cutting through the walnut. (We used a feather board to support the piece when making the final cuts.)

6. Return the table saw arbor to center, and mount a dado blade the same width as the inlay strip you plan to use (see the Buying Guide for our source of inlay). Referring

B

Finishing the angled cut using a feather board for support

Table saw fence

Third cuts

First cut

⅜"

Second cuts

3¹⁄₁₆"

³⁄₁₆"

⅛"

to the drawing *above*, position the rip fence ³⁄₁₆" from the inside edge of the dado set. Raise the blade to a height that equals the thickness of the inlay strip. Make the cut.

7. Make the second set of cuts ⅜" deep where shown in the drawing above. Remove the material left between those two dado cuts by making the third set of cuts, also shown above.

8. Use a single blade to make the final trim cut at a 10° angle along the front edge where shown in the drawing at *right.*

9. Glue the inlay in the shallow groove, and crosscut the lamination into two 5¹⁄₁₆" lengths.

10. Resaw a 1½"- wide strip of walnut to ⅜" thick. Crosscut two 2" long pieces from the strip for the pen holder blocks.

11. Sand a slight round-over along the top edges of each lamination and pen holder. Now, glue and clamp the pen holder blocks in positon. Drill a ¾"-deep hole at a slight angle in each pen holder to fit the barrel end of your favorite pen. Sand both holders smooth.

12. Apply a clear finish and glue a piece of felt to the bottom of each holder. Remove the brown paper backing from the backs of the Scotch Post-it Note Pads. Apply two strips of tape where shown on the Exploded View drawing at *left.* (The adhesive-backed pads stick better to the tape surface.)

Buying Guide
• **Inlay border.** Catalog no. B71, minimum length of 36". For current price, contact Constantine, 2050 Eastchester Rd., Bronx, NY 10461-2297.

Project Tool List
Tablesaw
  Dado blade or dado set
Portable drill
  Bit to fit pen
Finishing sander

Note: *We built the project using the tools listed. You may be able to substitute other tools or equipment for listed items you don't have. Additional common hand tools and clamps may be required to complete the project.*

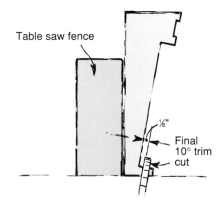

Table saw fence

⅛"

Final
10° trim
cut

HER FAVORITE THINGS

What woman wouldn't be thrilled to be given a beautiful necklace or bracelet handcrafted from wood? In addition to several pieces of jewelry, the following pages present a turned perfume decanter and an unusual hand mirror.

QUILT-LOOK HAND MIRROR

Once you grasp this finely crafted hand mirror, you'll know that it's more than just another vanity accessory. The quilt pattern evokes a country style. The smooth edges on the walnut frame almost beg to be touched. A builder of this treasured gift will not soon be forgotten.

Readying the walnut frame

Note: *You'll need ½" stock for this project. You can either resaw or plane thicker stock to size.*

1. Cut a piece of ½" walnut to 6x12" long for the mirror frame. (We planed down a piece of ¾" stock.) Mark reference lines on the walnut where shown on the drawing *below.*

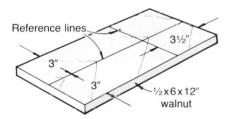

2. To make the template for routing the opening in the walnut, start by cutting a piece of ¼" hardboard to 6x8". Using carbon paper, center and transfer the router template outline (inside oval) and reference lines shown on the full-size half patterns at *right,* to the hardboard.

3. Carefully cut and sand the hardboard template opening to shape.

4. With double-faced tape, stick the template to the walnut, aligning the centerlines. Tape the walnut to a piece of scrap to avoid cutting into your workbench top when routing the opening.

5. Fit your router with a ⅝" bushing and a ½" straight bit. (Our bushing was too long, so we cut it with a hacksaw so it protruded a fraction less than ¼" below the

surface of the router base. (See the Buying Guide for our source of the router base and bushing.) With the bushing riding along the inside edge of the template, rout a ½" groove ⅜" deep in the walnut like that shown in step 1 of Routing the Opening drawings *below.* (We made several shallow passes and gradually increased the depth being routed. Trying to rout ⅜" deep in one pass may break the straight bit.)

6. Switch to a ¼" straight bit. Riding the bushing against the inside edge of the template, rout completely through the walnut and into the scrap base as shown in step 2. Separate the walnut from the scrap stock and template.

7. With carbon paper, trace the full-size patterns onto light cardboard. (Be sure to mark the reference lines so you can position the patterns correctly on the walnut.) Cut the cardboard patterns to shape. Tape the handle pattern
continued

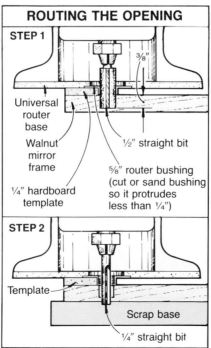

ROUTING THE OPENING

STEP 1
Universal router base
Walnut mirror frame
¼" hardboard template
½" straight bit
⅝" router bushing (cut or sand bushing so it protrudes less than ¼")
⅜"

STEP 2
Template
Scrap base
¼" straight bit

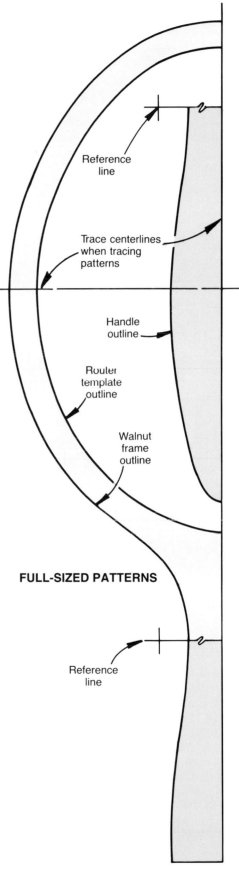

Reference line

Trace centerlines when tracing patterns

Handle outline

Router template outline

Walnut frame outline

FULL-SIZED PATTERNS

Reference line

QUILT-LOOK HAND MIRROR
continued

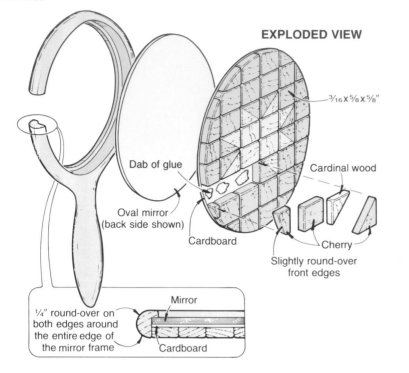

EXPLODED VIEW

3/16 X 5/8 X 5/8"

Dab of glue

Cardinal wood

Oval mirror
(back side shown)

Cardboard

Cherry

Slightly round-over
front edges

1/4" round-over on
both edges around
the entire edge of
the mirror frame

Mirror

Cardboard

piece to the frame pattern piece. Then, position the pattern on the walnut, align the reference lines with those on the walnut stock, and tape the pattern to the walnut. Now, using a bandsaw, cut the mirror frame to shape, remove the pattern, and then sand the cut edges smooth.

8. Chuck a 1/4" round-over bit into your table-mounted router. Rout a round-over along all the *outside* edges of the walnut frame. Hand-sand the entire frame (we wrapped sandpaper around a piece of foam to sand the rounded edges).

Laying-up the quilted insert

Note: You assemble the quilted insert oversize, and then cut and sand it to shape to ensure a tight fit within the routed opening

1. Plane or resaw a 24" length of 3/4" cherry and a 12" piece of 3/4" cardinal wood or another contrasting wood to 5/8" thick. Now, rip strips 3/16" wide (the lengths stated are extra long for safety when cutting).

2. Using a miter box, cut 20 cherry squares and 4 cardinal wood

squares (5/8X5/8"). With the remaining stock, miter-cut one end, and then crosscut as shown in the photo *below* to form the 16 trianglar pieces for the starlike center.

3. Cut a piece of cardboard to 3¾X5" (we used the backing from a writing tablet). Draw a horizontal and vertical centerline on the cardboard. Select four pieces of cardinal wood, and sand the top of each smooth. Then, sand a slight round-over on all four top edges of each square. Place a small dab of glue on the back of each, and glue them in position at the center of the cardboard, alternating the grain as shown on the Exploded View

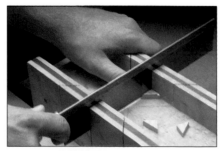

Cutting the triangular pieces to shape from the longer lengths.

drawing at *left*. (We used Super Glue; hotmelt adhesive also works.) Using the procedure just described, and working from the center out, glue the rest of the pieces in position on the cardboard to form your quilt insert.

4. Center the frame, rabbet side or front face down, over the quilted insert. Trace the rabbet outline onto the insert. Using a bandsaw, cut outside the marked line. Sand to the line until the insert fits snugly inside the rabbeted opening. Sand a slight round-over on the edges just cut.

Final assembly and finishing

1. Take the mirror frame to a glass shop, and have a mirror cut to size. Place the mirror in the opening. Run a bead of glue along the edge of the mirror, and glue the quilted insert in place. To avoid damaging the silvering, be careful not to get glue on the mirror back other than at the outside edge.

2. Mask off the mirror, and apply finish to the walnut frame and quilted insert. (We used lacquer.)

Buying Guide

• **Router guide bushing set.** Set has a universal router base plate that fits most popular round base routers. Also included are 5/16", 7/16", and 5/8"-diameter bushings. For current prices, contact Woodcraft Supply Corporation, 210 Wood County Industrial Park, P.O. Box 1686, Parkersburg, WV 26102, or call 800-225-1153 to order.

Project Tool List

Tablesaw
Bandsaw
Scrollsaw
Router
   Router table
   5/8" guide bushing
   Bits: 1/4" straight, 1/2" straight, 1/4" round-over

Note: We built the project using the tools listed. You may be able to substitute other tools or equipment for listed items you don't have. Additional common hand tools and clamps may be required to complete the project.

PERFUME DECANTER

Ten thousand lovers of perfume can't be wrong. That's how many of these stunning projects Myles Gilmer turned and sold before opening Myles Gilmer Wood Company in Portland, Oregon. Now, this ambitious craftsman spends less time turning, and more time selling his prized stock to bowl-hungry turners. See the Buying Guide for our source of glass perfume vials.

First, make a scrap faceplate

Myles starts by tracing the outline of his 3" metal faceplate onto a piece of 1"-thick stock. He cuts the piece round and screws the disc to his metal faceplate.

After mounting the faceplate assembly to the lathe, Myles starts the lathe, and locates and marks the center of the wood disc by marking concentric circles. Then, he drills a ⅝" hole ¾" deep at the marked centerpoint. Next, he cuts a piece of ⅝" dowel stock 5¼" long, and glues it squarely into the hole in the disc where shown on the drawing on *page 62* titled Set-Up for Turning the Cylinder.

Next comes the cylinder

After cutting three pieces and laminating them together for the cylinder (the lamination measures 1⅝x1⅝x4⅜"), Myles moves to the drill press, and drills a ⅝" hole 3½" deep centered into one end of the lamination. Fitting the lamination over the protruding dowel and
continued

EXPLODED VIEW

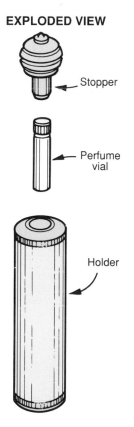

Stopper

Perfume vial

Holder

PERFUME DECANTER
continued

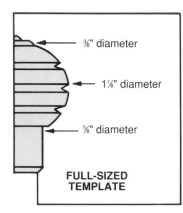

¾" diameter

1⅛" diameter

⅝" diameter

**FULL-SIZED
TEMPLATE**

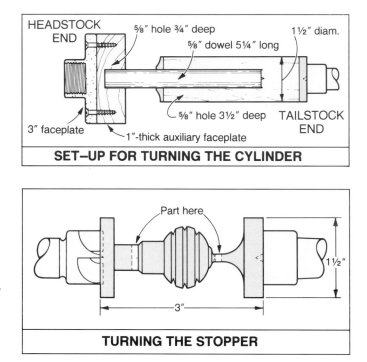

HEADSTOCK
END

⅝" hole ¾" deep

⅝" dowel 5¼" long

1½" diam.

3" faceplate

1"-thick auxiliary faceplate

⅝" hole 3½" deep

TAILSTOCK
END

SET–UP FOR TURNING THE CYLINDER

Part here

1½"

3"

TURNING THE STOPPER

sliding the tailstock against the bottom of the lamination come next. Then, Myles turns the lamination to a 1½" diameter with a 1" gouge. After sanding the cylinder smooth, he stops the lathe, and slides away the tailstock.

Shape the stopper

Myles cuts a block measuring 1½" square by 3" long for the stopper. After mounting it between centers where shown on the drawing *above right,* and turning it round, he uses a ¼" parting tool to create the beads and a ¼" roundnose for the coves.

"I take pride in making every stopper a bit different," Myles says. (See the full-sized template *above* to shape the stopper shown in the photograph on *page 61.*) "When making the fine V-cuts in a stopper, I use a ¼" parting tool. I lay the tool on its side on the tool rest, and scrape with the side of the tool rather than the flat face," he explains. Use the full-sized Template drawing for reference if you decide to make this particular stopper. (In making a few of our

own decorative stoppers in the *WOOD®* magazine shop, we found that a skew also works well for forming the stopper and making the V-cuts.)

Next, Myles turns the bottom portion of the stopper at a very slight taper for a snug fit into the ⅝" hole in the cylinder. Finally, he sands the stopper smooth, makes the parting cuts (see the stopper drawing *above* for reference), and seals the stopper and body with a clear finish.

Buying Guide
•**Glass ⅛-oz. perfume vials.** For current prices, contact Craft Supplies, 1287 E., 1120 S., Provo, UT 84606, or call 800-551-8876 or 801-373-0917 to order.

Project Tool List
Tablesaw
Bandsaw
Drill press
  ⅝" bit
Lathe
  3" faceplate
  Spur drive center
  Tail center
  1" gouge
  ¼" parting tool
  ¼" round nose

Note: *We built the project using the tools listed. You may be able to substitute other tools or equipment for listed items you don't have. Additional common hand tools and clamps may be required to complete the project.*

"JUST FOR HER" NECKLACE

J ewelry made of wood? You bet! This hardwood necklace will delight her and showcase your handicraft at the same time. We selected walnut and brass for our necklace, but don't let that limit your imagination. Use copper instead of brass for the inserts, or let the scraps of exotic woods you've been collecting determine the design.

1. Resaw, plane, or sand a 12" piece of scrap stock to 3/16" thick. (We used 1/4" stock and belt-sanded it down to 3/16".)

2. Transfer the shapes shown *below* onto the stock. Locate and mark the holes for the metal inserts where shown in the Front View drawing. Then, drill 1/8" holes in the outline of four smaller pieces and a 1/4" hole in the larger center piece. (We found it easier and safer to drill the holes now, rather than after cutting the pieces to shape.)

3. Epoxy and insert 1/4" brass or copper tubing into the hole in the center piece and 1/8" rod into the

holes of the other pieces. After the epoxy dries, sand or file the metal flush with the wood.

4. Cut the five walnut pieces to shape from the 12"-long stock. (We cut ours on a scrollsaw; a bandsaw also works well.)

5. Drill a 3/32" hole 1/8" from the top in the edge of each piece to accept a strand of leather lacing (available at Tandy and some hobby stores).

6. Using progressively finer grits of sandpaper, sand the necklace pieces smooth. Round-over the top of each slightly to prevent it from irritating the neck when worn. Finish with tung oil. (We applied the oil and rubbed it in with our fingers to the desired sheen.)

7. Insert the leather lacing through the holes, cut to the desired length, and tie behind the neck (or see a jeweler about obtaining a clasp).

Project Tool List
Scrollsaw or bandsaw
Portable drill or drill press
  Bits: 3/32", 1/8", 1/4"

Note: *We built the project using the tools listed. You may be able to substitute other tools or equipment for listed items you don't have. Additional common hand tools and clamps may be required to complete the project.*

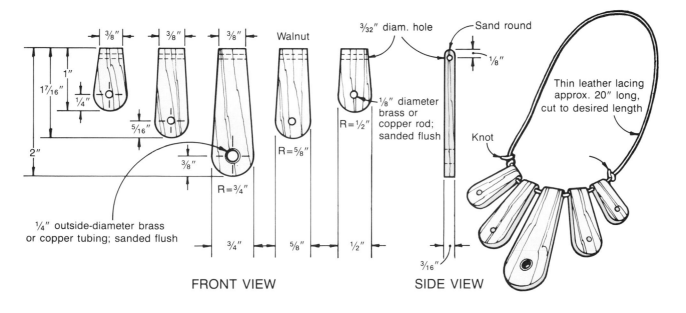

FRONT VIEW   SIDE VIEW

COUNTRY-STYLE SWAN NECKLACE

Here's a necklace project you'll want to dive into. It has that certain country charm not often found in jewelry. Using the full-sized photograph as a pattern and your scrollsaw or bandsaw, you're on your way to a sure-to-be-appreciated gift.

1. Using carbon paper, transfer the full-sized swan outline (as photographed on *this page*) to ⅜"-thick stock (we planed down ½" birch).

2. With a scrollsaw or a bandsaw fitted with a ⅛" blade, cut the swan to shape.

3. Chuck a ⅛" brad-point bit in your drill press. Then, clamp the swan piece in a handscrew clamp, position the swan below the bit, and drill a ⅛" hole through the head and neck where shown in the drawing *above center*.

4. Hand-sand the swan smooth, sanding a slight round-over along the front edges.

Note: Most hobby shops and craft stores stock the lacing and wooden beads (used for macrame) noted in the following steps and shown in the photo.

5. Paint the swan and the beads to the colors shown in the photograph (we used artist's acrylic paint).

FULL-SIZED PATTERN

6. Cut a piece of lacing (we used white rattail cord; narrow satin ribbon also would work) to 30" long. Thread the lacing through the ⅛" hole in the swan. Center the swan on the lacing, and tie one knot at the front of the head and another at the neck to keep the swan centered on the lacing. Tie two more knots 2" from the first ones where shown on the photograph. Next, add wooden beads onto the lacing on each side of the swan, and tie two more knots to hold the beads in place.

Project Tool List
Scrollsaw or bandsaw
Drill press
⅛" bit

Note: We built the project using the tools listed. You may be able to substitute other tools or equipment for listed items you don't have. Additional common hand tools and clamps may be required to complete the project.

AUTUMN DELIGHT WOODEN NECKLACE

Prepare to parade the autumn colors this year with this handcrafted necklace. Using our full-sized leaf patterns and your bandsaw or scrollsaw, you're minutes away from a finished project. Necklace designer Marie Fredrickson notes that this is one of her hottest-selling pieces.

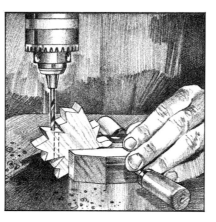

1. Using carbon paper or a photocopy, transfer the leaf patterns (one large and two small as displayed on this page) to ⅜" stock (we planed down ½" birch). If you want to eliminate staining the wood later, use scrap pieces of exotic woods.

2. With a bandsaw fitted with a ⅛" blade or a scrollsaw, cut the three leaves to shape.

3. Chuck a ⅛" brad-point bit into your drill press. Then, one at a time, clamp the leaves in a handscrew clamp, and drill a ⅛" hole through each as shown in the drawing *above center*. Use the lines indicating the hole locations on the full-sized photograph to align each leaf with the drill bit before drilling the holes.

4. Sand each leaf smooth. (We wrapped sandpaper around a nail file to sand the tight crevices. Stain, dye, or paint as desired (we mixed oil paints with natural Watco Danish Oil for our stain; you could also could stain them with thinned artist's acrylic paints).

Let the paint dry, and add a coat or two of clear finish.

5. Cut a piece of lacing (we used brown rattail cord; narrow

satin ribbon also would work) to 34" long. Thread the lacing through the ⅛" hole in the large maple leaf. Now, add an equal number of wooden beads onto the lacing on each side of the large leaf. Add the two smaller leaves,

and thread a few more beads next to them. Finally, tie together the lacing at the ends.

Note: *The lacing and wooden beads (like those used for macrame) are available at most hobby shops and craft supply stores.*

Project Tool List
Scrollsaw or bandsaw
Drill press
  ⅛" bit

Note: *We built the project using the tools listed. You may be able to substitute other tools or equipment for listed items you don't have. Additional common hand tools and clamps may be required to complete the project.*

SWEETHEART STICKPIN

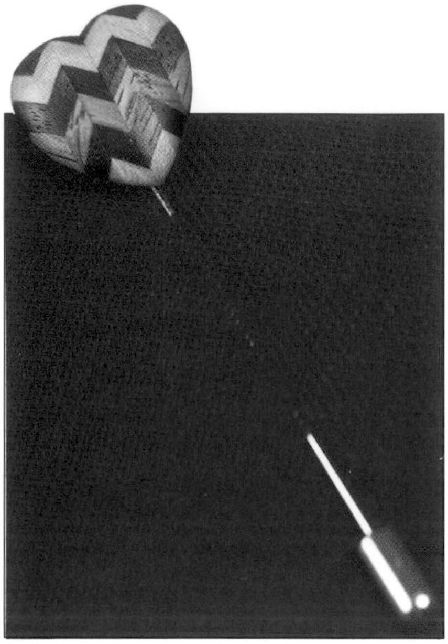

Out-of-the-ordinary jewelry always makes a welcome gift. This pin, laminated with woods from your scrap box, is a sweetheart to make, too—once you know how.

1. Rip ⅛"-wide strips from the edges of ¾"-thick boards 8" long to acquire the number and types of wood listed in the Bill of Materials, or choose your own combination. Glue and clamp the strips together alternating the wood types, as shown in step one of the photo *below*. Scrape off the excess glue.

2. Fit your bandsaw with a miter gauge set at 45° from center and a ¼" or larger blade having eight or more teeth per inch. Then, cut eight ⅛"-thick slices (see one slice in step two of the photo *below right*). Tape a piece of 80-grit sandpaper to a flat surface, and hand-sand both sides of each slice.

3. Glue and clamp two ⅛" slices together to form a chevron pattern as shown in step three of the photo. Repeat this process to make a total of four patterns.

4. Glue and clamp the four chevron patterns together to form the block (step four of the photo). Later, sand the top and bottom faces of the block smooth.

5. Position the fence on your bandsaw ¼" from the blade. Using a push block, cut ¼"-thick slabs from the laminated block. Then, as shown in step five of the photo, make a template, and draw a heart outline on each slab (use the full-sized Front View drawing, *below left*, to make the template).

6. Carefully cut the hearts to shape with a scrollsaw or bandsaw.

7. Round-over the top edge with a small rasp or sandpaper. As an option, use a power tool, such as a Dremel fitted with a ⅜" sanding drum. Finish-sand each heart.

8. Glue the pad of the stickpin to the back of the heart with epoxy. Rub in several coats of a penetrating oil finish, and wipe off the excess.

Buying Guide

• **Stickpins.** Gold finish, 2¾" long with bullet-type clutch. Stock no. 7872. Try your local hobby store or contact Meisel Hardware Specialties, P.O. Box 70, Mound, MN 55364-0070, or call 612-471-8550 or 800-441-9870 to order.

Project Tool List

Bandsaw
Scrollsaw

Note: *We built the project using the tools listed. You may be able to substitute other tools or equipment for listed items you don't have. Additional common hand tools and clamps may be required to complete the project.*

STICKPIN (Shown full size)

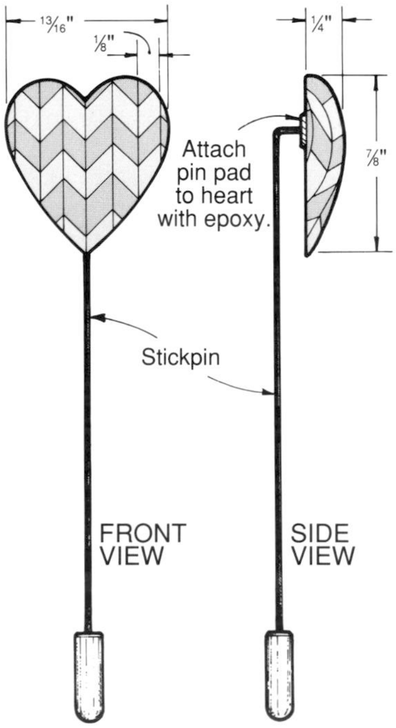
13⁄16"
⅛"
¼"
⅞"
Attach pin pad to heart with epoxy.
Stickpin
FRONT VIEW
SIDE VIEW

Bill of Materials

Part	Initial Size of Strips T	W	L	Mat.	Qty.
A	¾"	⅛"	8"	W	4
B	¾"	⅛"	8"	M	2
C	¾"	⅛"	8"	O	1

Material Key: W—walnut, M—maple, O—oak
Supplies: masking tape, epoxy, finish

LAMINATION AND CUTTING SEQUENCE

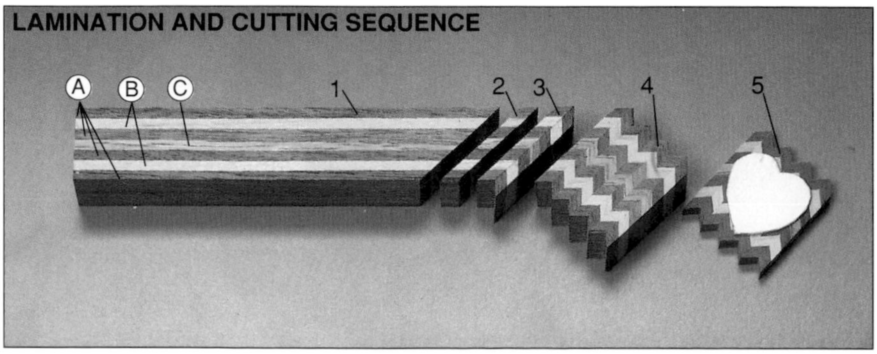
A
B
C
1
2
3
4
5

DESIGNER EARRINGS

Bonnie Klein of Renton, Washington, excels in turning small items. Her idea for turned jewelry evolved from a desire to turn earrings that didn't look like miniature spindles. We think you'll agree that her method of turning tiny bowls, and then cutting and sanding them to shape, creates earrings that are anything but ordinary.

First, she makes a scrap faceplate

Bonnie starts by marking a 3"-diameter circle on a piece of 1½"-thick pine, and then cuts it to shape on the bandsaw. To mount the scrap faceplate to the lathe, Bonnie drills a ¾"-deep hole at the centerpoint. The hole measures ¹⁄₁₆" smaller in diameter than the outside diameter of the headstock spindle on her lathe. Rotating the headstock spindle by hand, the industrious turner threads the pine faceplate onto the spindle. Next, she starts the lathe, turns the pine to a 1¾" diameter, and squares the face. With the lathe running, she marks concentric circles about ¹⁄₁₆" apart on the face of the faceplate. The circles aid when centering the turning stock later.

Now, Bonnie turns and finishes the small bowl

For the earring blanks, Bonnie marks and band-saws pieces 1½" in diameter from ¾" or thicker stock. Using the concentric circles on the scrap faceplate, she centers and glues the earring blank to the faceplate. Bonnie turns the earring blank round and trues up the face.

Turning a shallow depression ⅜" deep—in the face of the earring blank with a ¼" spindle gouge comes next. Bonnie then turns the back of the piece with a ¼" skew chisel to form a small bowl as shown in the drawing *below*. "I leave a ⅛"-diameter stub to hold the bowl on the lathe for sanding and finishing," notes Bonnie. "After sanding, I use a mixture of shellac, alcohol, and linseed oil on some of the pieces. Some woods, such as cocobolo and kingwood, look best with just an

application of wax." Then, as shown *below*, she parts the miniature bowl from the lathe, hand-sands, and applies a finish to the unfinished area left by the stub.

The final task—cutting and shaping the earrings

Bonnie cuts the bowl in half on a scrollsaw, and disc-sands the cut edge to shape the earring. By holding the earring against the disc at different angles, she can vary the final shape. Hand-sanding the shaped edges comes next, followed by drilling a ¹⁄₃₂" hole, and attaching the ear wire. "Pay close attention to how you want the earrings to hang," Bonnie says. "There's a definite left and right earring. Adjust the direction the earrings hang by twisting the lower rings."

Buying Guide
•**Fishhook earrings.** Gold earring wire, stock no. 3389. Gold jump ring, stock no. 3392. For current prices, contact Meisel Hardware Specialties, P.O. Box 70, Mound, MN 55364-0700, or call 612-471-8550 or 800-441-9870 to order.

Project Tool List
Bandsaw
Scrollsaw
Drill press
   Bit: see text
Lathe
   ¼" gouge, ¼" skew
   ⅛" parting tool

Note: *We built the project using the tools listed. You may be able to substitute other tools or equipment for listed items you don't have. Additional common hand tools and clamps may be required to complete the project.*

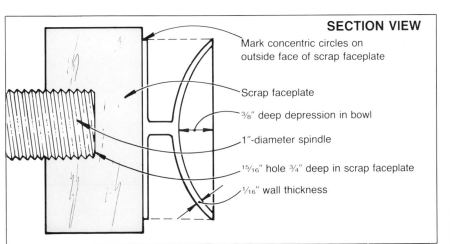

SECTION VIEW

Mark concentric circles on outside face of scrap faceplate

Scrap faceplate

⅜" deep depression in bowl

1"-diameter spindle

¹⁵⁄₁₆" hole ¾" deep in scrap faceplate

¹⁄₁₆" wall thickness

BRING ON THE BRACELETS

By now, all of you turners out there probably are aware that we'll go to great lengths to find out-of-the-ordinary projects for you to tackle. Here, we're disclosing the secrets of woodturner Ab Odnoken from the prairie city of Saskatoon in Saskatchewan. After spending his days as a postal officer, Ab heads to his lathe at night to turn items such as these bracelets for his four daughters and two daughters-in-law.

Start by forming the bracelet blank

This industrious Canadian turner begins by marking a 3¾"-diameter circle on a piece of ½" scrap stock with a compass. When he runs low on ½" stock, he resaws thicker stock to size on his bandsaw. Then, he mounts a circle cutter to his drill press, centers the pilot bit directly over the compass centerpoint used to mark the circle, and cuts the bracelet's interior. For safety, Ab holds the stock with a handscrew clamp when cutting to prevent it from spinning with the cutter. "I cut the opening to 2¾" in diameter for large wrists, and 2¼" for smaller wrists," Ab notes. "Next, I cut the marked circumference of the bracelet blank to shape with a bandsaw, and sand the interior smooth with a drum sander."

Turn the bracelet to shape on the mandrel

After shaping a softwood mandrel between centers (see the drawing at *right)*, Ab slides the bracelet blank onto the mandrel, and twists the blank clockwise to lock it snugly onto the tapered stock. Then, he uses a ½" gouge to shape the round-over on the narrower end (end nearest the tailstock) of the mandrel. (See

the full-sized template at *right* for help.)

Ab then slides the bracelet off the mandrel. He turns it over, slides it back on the mandrel, twists it onto the mandrel to lock it in place, and shapes the other side. Next, he sands the bracelet smooth, removes it from the mandrel, and

hand sands a slight round-over on the interior edges. "To finish the exotic woods such as ebony, cocobolo, and cardinal wood, a good waxing is all that's needed," Ab says. "For the softer and domestic woods, I use Minwax tung oil or polyurethane."

Project Tool List
Bandsaw
Drill press
   Circle cutter
   Drum sander
Lathe
   Spur drive center
   Tail center
   ½" gouge

Note: *We built the project using the tools listed. You may be able to substitute other tools or equipment for listed items you don't have. Additional common hand tools and clamps may be required to complete the project.*

FULL-SIZED TEMPLATE

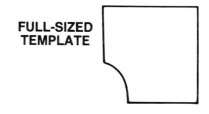

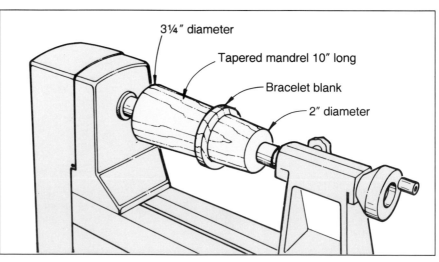

3¼" diameter
Tapered mandrel 10" long
Bracelet blank
2" diameter

QUALITY-CRAFTED PENDULUM CRADLE

Here's a cradle that's sure to be passed on from generation to generation. Made of durable ash, the cradle features a simple rocking mechanism that offers a soothing solution to the cries of restless babies. What better way to express your love and pride in honor of the newborn?

Laminating and shaping the basket end panels

1. To make the basket ends, cut two A's and eight B's to the sizes listed in the Bill of Materials on *page 70.*

2. Dry-clamp each basket end panel together, with the bottom edges of all parts flush. Next, mark the dowel locations where dimensioned on the drawing at *right.*

3. Remove the clamps and drill ⅜" holes ¹³⁄₁₆" deep where marked (we used a doweling jig). Glue, dowel, and clamp the pieces together for each end panel. Once clamped, check them for flatness with a straightedge. If necessary,

loosen the clamps and flatten against the pipes of bars of the clamps.

4. Mark a centerline on one of the end panels where shown on the Basket End Panel Shape drawing on *page 70.* Then, lay out the panel's shape as shown in the same drawing. Cut and sand the end panel to shape. (We cut ours on a bandsaw, cutting slightly outside the marked line. Then, we belt-sanded to the marked line for a near perfect final shape). Use this panel as a template to shape the second panel. Now, cut and sand that panel to shape.

5. Lay out and mark the center for the ⅜" dowel holes and the ¼" screw hole on one of the basket end panels using the dimensions on the drawing. Using double-faced tape, tape the two ends together, face to face, with the edges flush. Drill the ¼" and ⅜" holes through both end panels at the marked centerpoints, backing the panels with scrap wood to prevent chip- *continued*

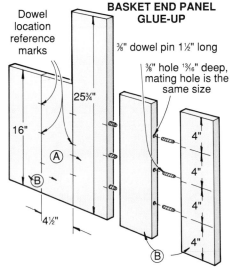

BASKET END PANEL GLUE-UP

Dowel location reference marks

⅜" dowel pin 1½" long

⅜" hole ¹³⁄₁₆" deep, mating hole is the same size

25¾"

16"

4½"

4"

4"

4"

4"

Ⓐ

Ⓑ

QUALITY-CRAFTED PENDULUM CRADLE
continued

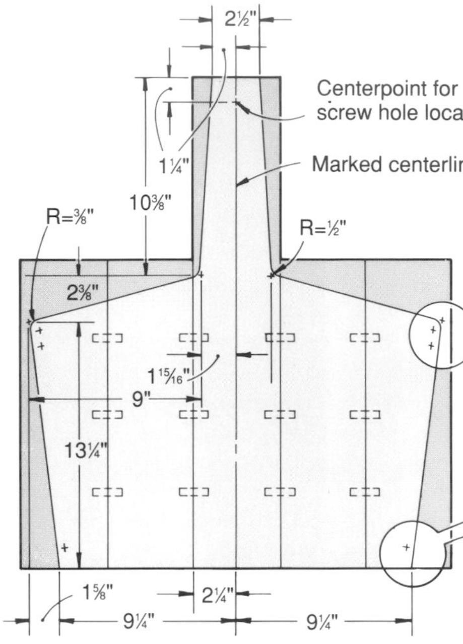
2½"
Centerpoint for ¼" screw hole location
1¼"
Marked centerline
10⅜"
R=⅜"
R=½"
2⅜"
1¹⁵⁄₁₆"
9"
13¼"
1⅝"
2¼"
9¼"
9¼"

BASKET END PANEL

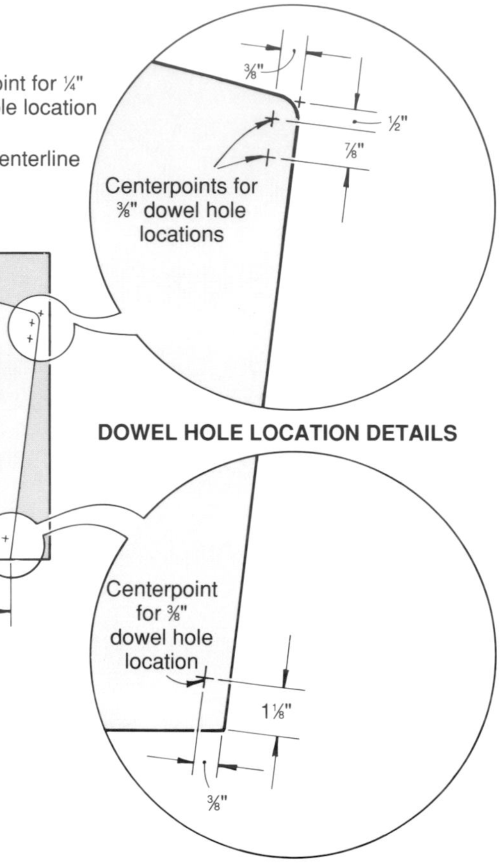
⅜"
½"
⅞"
Centerpoints for ⅜" dowel hole locations
Centerpoint for ⅜" dowel hole location
1⅛"
⅜"

DOWEL HOLE LOCATION DETAILS

out. Separate the ends and countersink the ¼" holes on the *inside* face of each end panel (see the Rocking Joint detail *opposite*). Now, drill a ⅜" hole ¼" deep centered over the ¼" hole on the *outside* face of each end to accept the ¼" T-nut.

Now for the basket sides

1. Cut the upper and lower rails (C) to size. Using the Rail details *opposite* for reference, rout the ¼" and ⅜" round-overs along the edges of each rail where shown.

2. Mount a ¼" dado set to your table saw, and cut a ¼" groove ¼" deep centered along the bottom edge of the top rails and the top edge of the bottom rails. Now, tilt the blade 8° from center, and cut a ¼" groove ¼" deep in each bottom rail where shown in the Rail details.

3. To make the slats (D), cut several ¾"- thick boards 10" in length. Now, rip 34—¼"-thick strips from the edges of the boards to obtain ¼X¾"-wide slats. (When ripping the slats, we would cut three or four slats on the bandsaw, stop and joint the edge being cut, and then cut three or four more. You can also cut them on a table saw and eliminate the jointing.) Sand the slats smooth.

4. To form the spacers (E, F), start by resawing four strips ¼X⅜X24" long from thicker stock. Set a stop and cut 8 spacers (E) 2" long. Now, cut 64 of the 1" spacers (F).

5. Measure and mark the center (between the two ends) of each rail. Then, mark a centerline down one face of two of the slats. As shown in the photo *above right,* glue and position one of the marked slats in the groove, aligning the centerline mark with the centerline on the bottom rail. Working from the center to the ends, glue the slats and spacers in position, checking that each slat aligns square with the rail. Save the long spacers for the ends of the groove, and trim them to length after they are installed.

continued

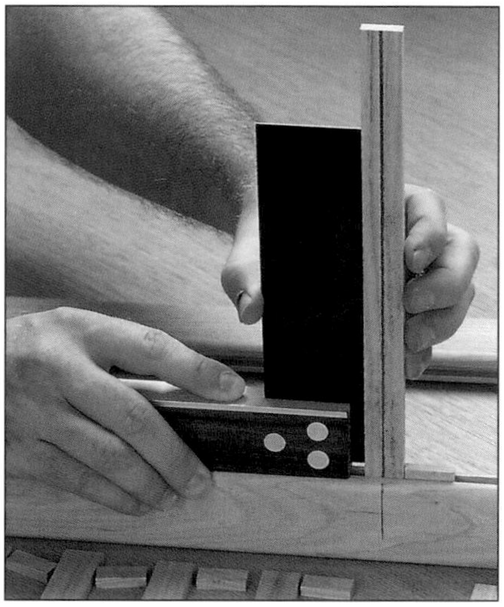

Center and square the middle slat with the bottom rail.

Bill of Materials

Part	Finished Size* T	W	L	Mat.	Qty.
BASKET					
A ends	¾"	4½"	25¾"	WA	2
B ends	¾"	4½"	16"	WA	8
C lower rails	¾"	2"	31"	WA	4
D slats	¼"	¾"	10"	WA	34
E* spacers	¼"	⅜"	1⅛"	WA	8
F spacers	¼"	⅜"	1"	WA	64
G bottom	¼"	17⅝"	31"	H	1
H cleats	⅜"	⅜"	17"	WA	2
CRADLE SUPPORTS					
I uprights	1¹⁄₁₆"	4¼"	30½"	WA	2
J bases	1¹⁄₁₆"	5¼"	24¼"	WA	2
K cross member	1¹⁄₁₆"	3¼"	33"	WA	1

*Part marked with an * is cut larger initially, and then trimmed to finished size. Please read the instructions before cutting.

Material Key: WA—white ash, H—hardboard.
Supplies: ⅜" dowel pins 1½" long, double-faced tape, ⅜" oak dowel stock, 2—¼" brass flathead machine screws 1½" long, 2—¼" T-nuts, ¼" brass flat washers, #6X1" flathead wood screws, masking tape, polyurethane.

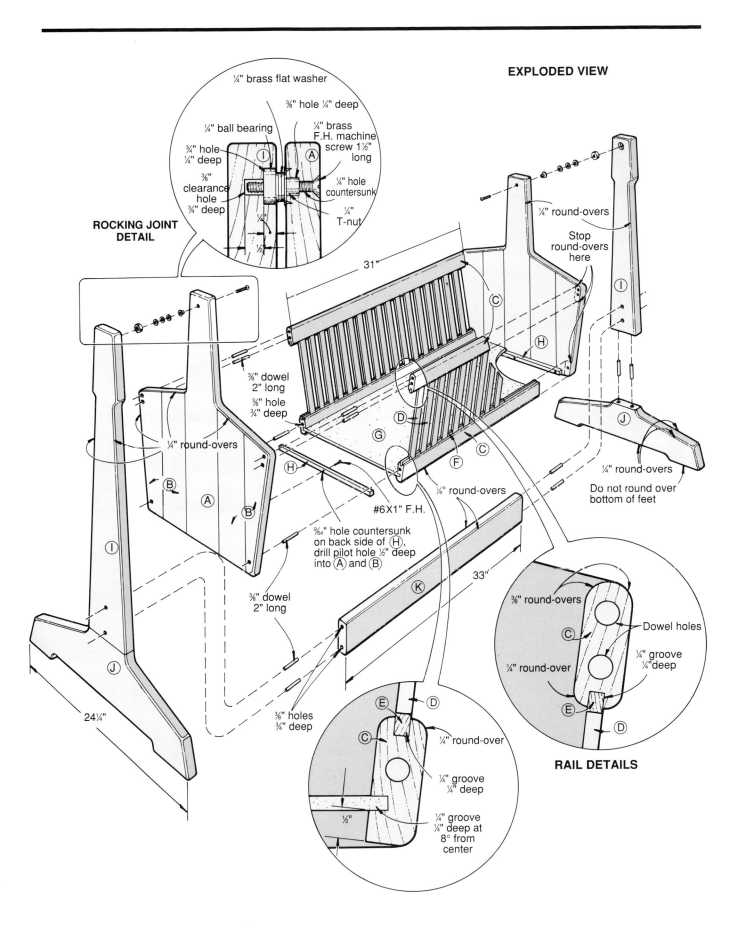

EXPLODED VIEW

ROCKING JOINT DETAIL

¼" brass flat washer

⅜" hole ¼" deep

¼" ball bearing

¼" brass F.H. machine screw 1½" long

¾" hole ¼" deep

Ⓘ Ⓐ

⅜" clearance hole ¾" deep

¼" hole countersunk

¼" T-nut

¼"

½"

31"

¼" round-overs

Stop round-overs here

Ⓒ

Ⓗ

Ⓘ

⅜" dowel 2" long

⅜" hole ¾" deep

¼" round-overs

Ⓑ

Ⓐ

Ⓑ

Ⓗ

Ⓓ

Ⓖ

Ⓕ

Ⓒ

Ⓙ

¼" round-overs

Do not round over bottom of feet

Ⓘ

#6X1" F.H.

⁹⁄₆₄" hole countersunk on back side of Ⓗ, drill pilot hole ½" deep into Ⓐ and Ⓑ

⅜" dowel 2" long

Ⓙ

24¼"

Ⓚ

33"

⅜" holes ¾" deep

⅜" round-overs

Ⓒ

Dowel holes

¼" round-over

¼" groove ¼" deep

Ⓔ

Ⓓ

RAIL DETAILS

Ⓔ Ⓓ

Ⓒ

¼" round-over

¼" groove ¼" deep

½"

¼" groove ¼" deep at 8° from center

QUALITY-CRAFTED PENDULUM CRADLE
continued

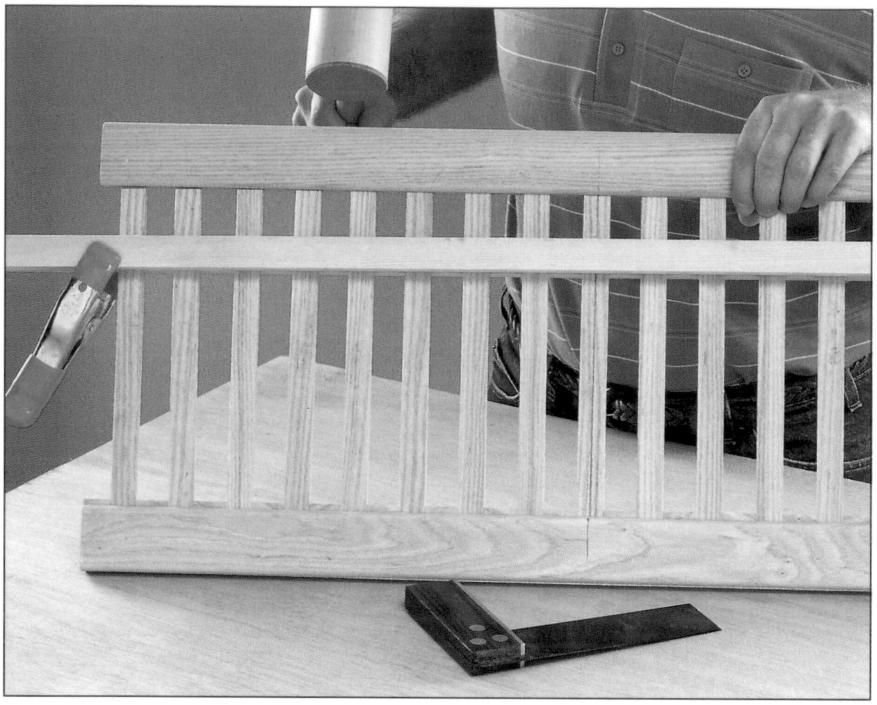

Align the top rail with the marked middle slat, and then fit the rest of the ash slats into the groove in the top rail.

Repeat this process with the second bottom rail.

6. Clamp a scrap strip on each side of the slats to align them as shown in the photo *above.* Now, run a bead of glue along the groove in each top rail. Center the top rail on the center slat, and tap it onto the ends of the slats as shown in the photo. Next, flip the assembly over to keep the glue in the groove from running down the slats. Again, starting at the center, glue the spacers in position, and trim the end spacers flush. Repeat this procedure for the second basket side.

Assembling the basket

1. Cut the hardboard basket bottom (G) and the two cleats (H) to size.

2. Run a bead of glue in the ¼" groove in each bottom rail. Insert the basket bottom between the two bottom rails. Dry-clamp the rails in position between the basket end panels, centering the rails over the ⅜" dowel holes in the panels. Make sure the rails are flush with the outside edge of the panels. (We used a bar clamp at each corner to hold the rails firmly in position.)

3. Using the previously drilled dowel holes as guides, drill ⅜" holes ¾" deep into the end of each rail. (To do this, we first centered a brandpoint bit inside the hole, turned the drill on, and then drilled into the rails. If you start the drill and then try to insert and align the spinning bit in the guide hole, it tends to drill the hole oversize and off-center.) Later, after the glue holding the hardboard bottom in position has dried, remove the clamps.

4. Mark the routing start and stop location on the end panels, using the Exploded View drawing on *page 71* as a guide. Repeat this process with the other end panel. Rout a ¼" round-over completely around the outside face of each end panel. Then, rout a ¼" round-over on the inside face of each panel, stopping where marked.

5. Cut twelve ⅜X2" dowels from oak dowel stock. Form a glue groove in all but the end (which is exposed) of each dowel to prevent forcing the glue from the dowel hole. (We held the dowel in a hand screw and formed the groove with a sharp chisel.)

6. Apply a small amount of glue to the ends of the rails and in the dowel holes. Position the end panels against the rails. Glue and tap the dowels through the basket ends and into the rails. Now, clamp the doweled assembly together. Later, trim and sand the dowels flush with the face of each end panel.

7. To attach the cleats (H), stand the basket on end. Drill and countersink holes to the sizes stated

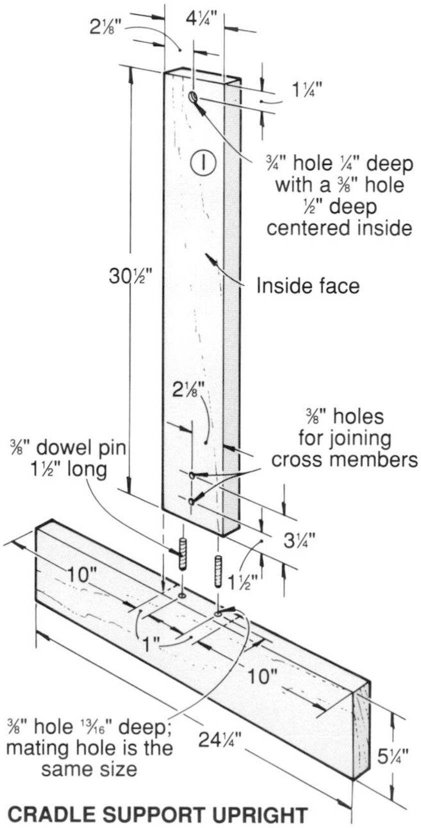
2⅛"
4¼"
1¼"
I
¾" hole ¼" deep with a ⅜" hole ½" deep centered inside
30½"
Inside face
2⅛"
⅜" holes for joining cross members
⅜" dowel pin 1½" long
3¼"
10"
1½"
1"
10"
⅜" hole 13/16" deep; mating hole is the same size
24¼"
5¼"

CRADLE SUPPORT UPRIGHT

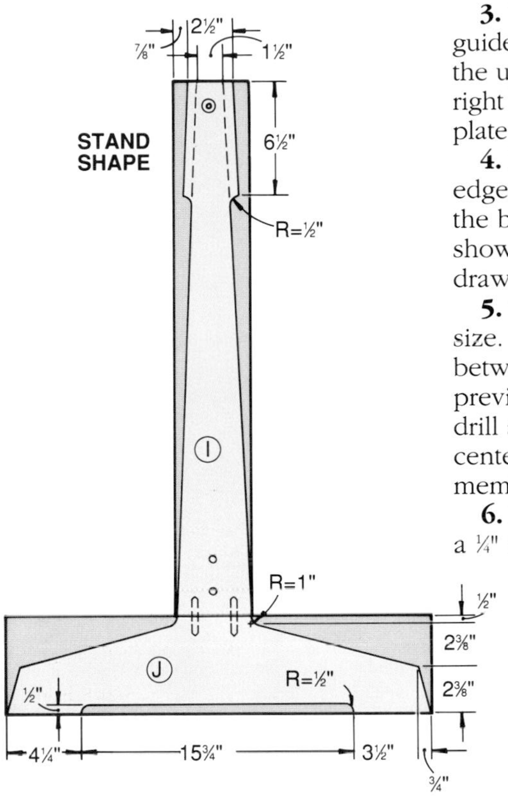
STAND SHAPE
2½"
⅞"
1½"
6½"
R=½"
I
R=1"
J
R=½"
½"
4¼"
15¾"
3½"
2⅜"
2⅜"
½"
¾"

on the Exploded View drawing, and glue and screw the cleats in position.

8. Sand the basket assembly smooth.

Basket support assembly

1. Using 1 1/16" stock, cut the vertical parts (I) and the bases (J) to the sizes listed in the Bill of Materials.

2. Using the drawing *opposite* as a guide, mark the location of all the holes shown. Then, drill each hole to the size and depth specified. Now, glue, dowel, and clamp each upright together.

3. Using the drawing *at left* as a guide, lay out the shape of one of the uprights. Cut and sand the upright to shape. Now, use it as a template to make an identical upright.

4. Rout a ¼" round-over on all edges of each upright, except on the bottom edges of the feet where shown on the Exploded View drawing.

5. Cut the cross member (K) to size. Dry-clamp it in position between the uprights. Using the previously drilled holes as guides, drill a pair of ⅜" holes ⅞" deep centered on each end of the cross member.

6. Remove the clamps, and rout a ¼" round-over along the four edges (but not the ends) of the cross member.

7. Glue, dowel, and clamp the cross member between the uprights checking for square. Later, sand the dowels flush.

Final Assembly

1. Tap a ¼" ball bearing into each ¾" hole in each upright. (See the Buying Guide for our source of bearings.) Tap a ¼" T-nut into the ⅜" hole in each basket end panel.

2. To check the fit of the basket in the support assembly, insert a machine screw through the inside face of each baset end panel, and thread it through the T-nut as shown on the Rocking Joint detail on *page 71.* Using a helper to hold the basket between the uprights, continue threading both screws through the T-nuts, Then, add ¼" brass washers for spacers, and thread the screws through the bearings. Thread each screw until the head is flush with the inside face of the basket end.

3. Remove the machine screws to separate the basket from the support assembly. Mask off the bearings and T-nuts. Touch-up sand if necessary and apply the stain and finish (we left ours unstained and applied several coats of polyurethane).

4. Remove the masking from the bearings and T-nuts, and reattach the basket to the stand.

Buying Guide

- **Cradle pad.** 17x31" vinyl-covered foam pad. For current prices, contact Sleepland, 4412 N.E. 14th, Des Moines, IA 50313, or call 515-262-2705.
- **¼" ball bearings (2).** ¾" outside diameter, ¼" inside diameter, stock no. BRBR4A-22. For current prices, contact Standard Bearings, P.O. Box 823, Des Moines, IA 50304, or call 800-554-8123 or 515-262-5261.

Project Tool List

Tablesaw
  Dado blade or dado set
Bandsaw
Drill
  Doweling jig
Drill press
  Bits: ¼", 9/64", ⅜", ¾"
Router
  Bits: ¼" round-over,
    ⅜" round-over
Belt sander
Finishing sander

Note: *We built the project using the tools listed. You may be able to substitute other tools or equipment for listed items you don't have. Additional common hand tools and clamps may be required to complete the project.*

FOR THE KITCHEN WITH LOVE

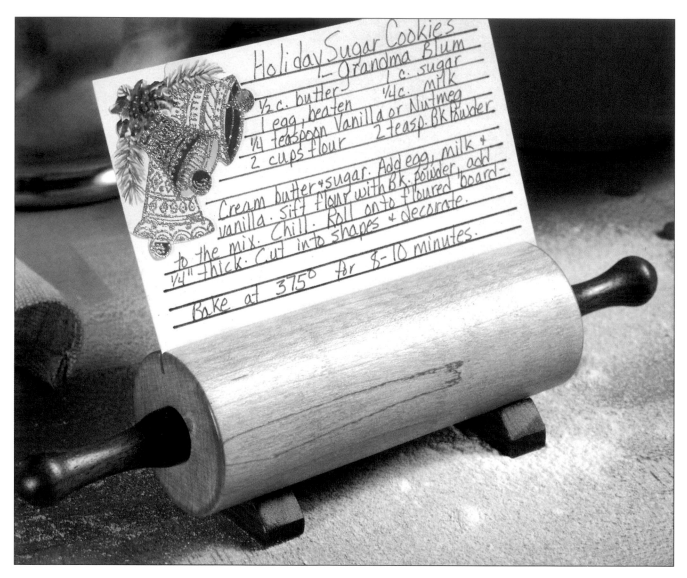

Wood is a natural in the kitchen, as you'll see in the projects that follow. These gifts for the cook range from a handy pizza paddle to a clever noodle cutter, from a handsome cutlery case to a matching set of steak knives.

ROLLING-PIN RECIPE-CARD HOLDER

Typically, recipe cards receive plenty of abuse while being used for meal preparation. And over time, spills and splatters take their toll. Keep your recipe cards up and out of harm's way with this novel project.

Turn the barrel, and cut the kerf

1. Cut a 5½" length from a 2" maple turning square for the barrel (A). If you don't have stock this thick, laminate thinner pieces to size. Draw diagonals on each end to find center. Punch a small indentation at each marked centerpoint, and mount the stock between centers on your lathe. Turn the barrel to a 1¾" diameter, and use a parting tool to square the ends.

2. With the barrel still mounted between centers, sand it smooth.

3. As shown in photo A *above right,* secure the barrel in a hand-screw clamp. Center the bit (we used a brad-point) over the indented centerpoint, and drill a ½" hole ½" deep. Repeat on the opposite end.

4. Clamp the barrel in a woodworkers vise, and use a backsaw to cut a ¹⁄₁₆" kerf ¼" deep to hold the recipe card later. Finish-sand the barrel.

Shape the handles with a drum sander

1. Cut two 3⅜"-long pieces from ½"-diameter walnut dowel for the rolling-pin handles (B).

2. Chuck the top 1" of one dowel section into your drill press. Fit your portable drill with a 2" drum sander. With the drill press running at about 750 rpm, sand a concave shape to each handle as shown in photo B *below right* and on the full-sized Handle pattern. Hand-sand the very end of the handle to shape.

Add the bases and finish

1. Transfer the base pattern shown *below* to ½" walnut stock. Cut two bases (C) to shape. Sand smooth.

2. Glue a handle in each end of the barrel. Glue and clamp the bases to the barrel where shown in the Exploded View drawing *below.*

3. Remove any excess glue and sand smooth. Apply a clear finish (we used lacquer).

BASE

Ⓒ

FULL-SIZED BASE

Find center and bore a ½" hole ½" deep into both ends of the barrel.

With a portable drill and drill press running, sand the handles to shape.

Project Tool List
Tablesaw
Bandsaw or scrollsaw
Drill press
Portable drill
   Drum sander
   ½" bit
Lathe
   Spur drive center
   Tail center
   ½" gouge
   ⅛" parting tool

Note: *We built the project using the tools listed. You may be able to substitute other tools or equipment for listed items you don't have. Additional common hand tools and clamps may be required to complete the project.*

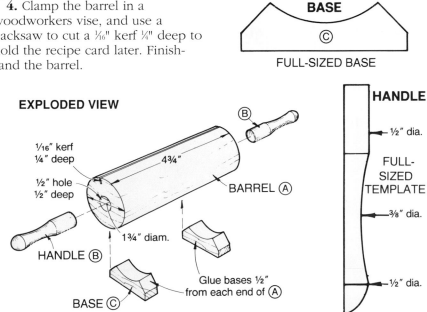

EXPLOSED VIEW

Ⓑ

¹⁄₁₆" kerf
¼" deep

4¾"

½" hole
½" deep

BARREL Ⓐ

HANDLE Ⓑ

1¾" diam.

BASE Ⓒ

Glue bases ½"
from each end of Ⓐ

HANDLE

½" dia.

FULL-SIZED TEMPLATE

⅜" dia.

½" dia.

MAKE 'EM IN A DASH SHAKERS

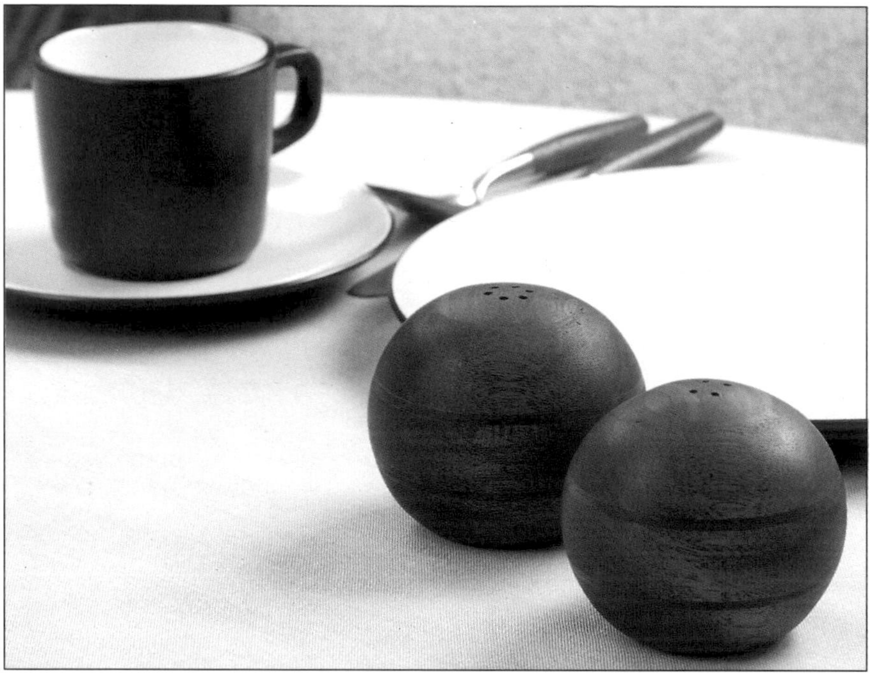

Spice up somebody's table setting with these palm-sized mahogany and walnut shakers. They're nice to look at, nice to handle, and you can turn them out quicker than a wink.

1. Rip and crosscut parts A, B, and C to the size listed in the Bill of Materials. For part B you need ⅛" walnut stock. You can either resaw and sand thicker material to ⅛" or plane thicker stock to size.

2. Using the Side View drawing *below left* as a reference, glue and clamp the walnut and mahogany pieces into two equal-size stacks, keeping the edges flush. We alternated the grain direction of each layer, as shown in the Side View drawing, for stability and eye appeal.

3. After the glue has dried, scrape off the excess. Find the centerpoint on the top of each lamination by marking diagonals from corner to corner. (Although it's not essential, we used a bandsaw to cut the laminations to rough shape prior to turning them.)

Bill of Materials

Part	Size T	Size W	Size L	Mat.	Qty.
FOR TWO SHAKERS					
A	¾"	3¼"	3¼"	HM	6
B	⅛"	3¼"	3¼"	W	4
C	¾"	3¼"	3¼"	W	2

Material Key: HM—Honduras mahogany, W—walnut.
Supplies: polyurethane, two #10 corks that taper from 1" to ¾" (available at most hobby stores and some hardware stores).

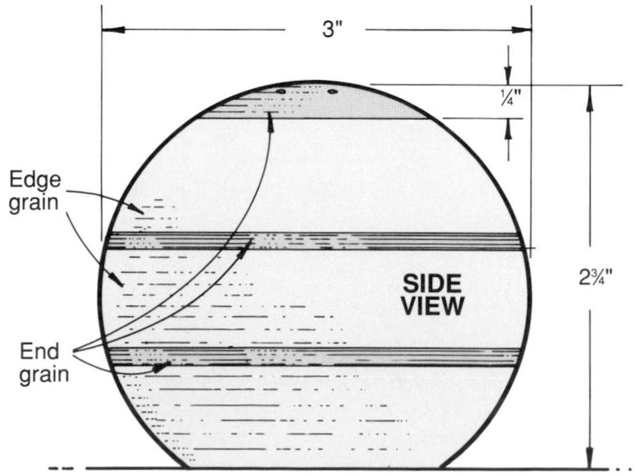
3"
¼"
2¾"
Edge grain
End grain
SIDE VIEW

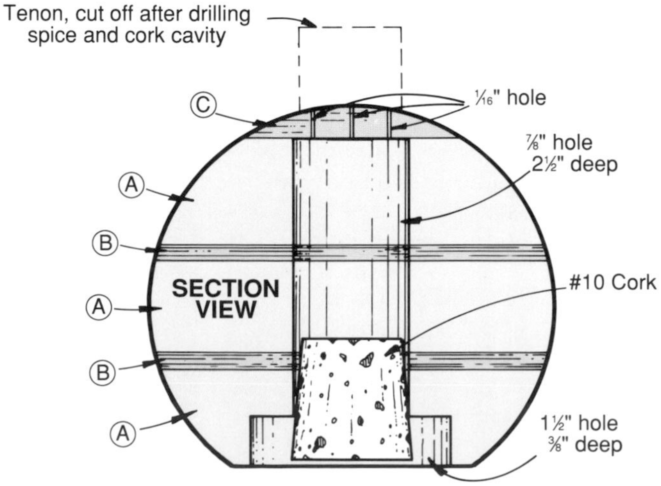
Tenon, cut off after drilling spice and cork cavity
C
A
B
A
B
A
1⁄16" hole
⅞" hole 2½" deep
SECTION VIEW
#10 Cork
1½" hole ⅜" deep

4. Mount one of the walnut and mahogany laminations on the lathe with the walnut against the tailstock. (We mounted each lamination between centers, as shown in the photo *above*)

5. Using a large gouge, round-down the laminated block to the largest cylinder size possible. (We started with a sharp gouge to ensure a good cut and minimal chipping.)

6. Bore a ¾" hole through a piece of ¾" scrap material (this board will serve as a mounting block later when the holes are being drilled in the shakers). Now, lay out the tenon (walnut end of the block) and turn it down to ¾" diameter with a parting tool. Check the diameter with a pair of outside calipers as you turn it down. At just a hair over ¾", stop the lathe, slide the tailstock and turned stock away from the live center, and check the fit of the tenon in the ¾" hole you bored in the mounting block. Turn until the tenon fits snugly in the hole.

7. Using a piece of cardboard or hardboard and the Side View

drawing as a reference, outline the profile of the finished shakers on it. Cut the profile template to shape.

8. Turn the stock down to about ⅟₁₆" over size, stopping the lathe periodically and checking the shape against the template as shown in photo at *left*. (We marked lines on the template to correspond with the walnut stripes in the shaker for a more accurate contour.) Finish-sand the shaker to size.

9. Remove the shaker from the lathe and fit the tenon in the ¾" hole in the mounting block. Center and clamp the shaker and mounting block to the drill press (see the photo *below*). Using a 1½" flat-bottomed bit (we used a Forstner), bore a recess ⅜" deep in the nearly completed shaker. Without moving the shaker and mounting block, change to a ⅞" flat-bottomed bit and drill to a depth of 2½".

HOLE PATTERN

Salt

Pepper

R = ¼"

10. Remove the shaker from the mounting block and drill press, saw off the tenon, and sand the top end to shape. (When cutting the tenon off the end, we left on about ⅛" of the tenon, and then sanded the top to shape.)

11. Repeat steps 4 through 10 to fashion the other shaker.

12. Lay out the hole pattern on the top of each shaker and drill ⅟₁₆" holes (see the Hole Pattern drawing *above* for help with this).

13. Apply several coats of finish, being careful not to clog the holes. (We finished ours with polyurethane to minimize the difference in color between end and edge grain.)

Project Tool List
Tablesaw
Bandsaw
Drill press
   Bits: ⅟₁₆" , ¾", ⅞", 1½"
Belt sander
Lathe
   Spur drive center
   Tail center
   ½", ¾" gouges
   ⅛" parting tool

Note: *We built the project using the tools listed. You may be able to substitute other tools or equipment for listed items you don't have. Additional common hand tools and clamps may be required to complete the project.*

SPICED-UP NAPKIN HOLDER

Great projects deserve attention. This helpful dining accessory will get rave reviews because it organizes three mealtime essentials into an attractive angular package. So, tie on a shop apron and follow our how-to recipe.

Build the base first

1. From ½" oak, cut the base parts (A, B) and uprights (C) to the sizes listed in the Bill of Materials.

EXPLODED VIEW

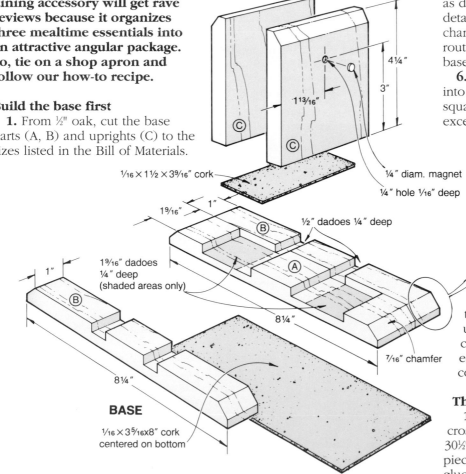

1/16 × 1 1/2 × 3 9/16" cork

¼" diam. magnet
¼" hole 1/16" deep

4 1/4"
3"
1 13/16"

½" dadoes ¼" deep

1 9/16"   1"

7/16"
3/16"

CHAMFER DETAIL

1 9/16" dadoes ¼" deep (shaded areas only)

1"

8 1/4"

7/16" chamfer

8 1/4"

BASE

1/16 × 3 5/16x8" cork centered on bottom

2. With a square, mark the locations and then cut a pair of 1⁵/₁₆" dadoes ¼" deep for the shaker recesses in part A where dimensioned on the Top View drawing *opposite*. Then, sand the dado bottoms smooth.

3. Glue and clamp the base pieces (A, B) with the edges and ends flush. Immediately remove any glue squeeze-out in the dadoed recesses. Later, remove the clamps, scrape off the excess glue, and trim about ³/₃₂" off each end for flush ends.

4. Mark the location of the dadoes for the uprights (C) where dimensioned on the Top View drawing. As shown on the drawing, cut the dadoes to the same depth as the previously dadoed recesses.

5. Chamfer both ends of the base (A, B) and one end of each upright as dimensioned on the Chamfer detail *below*. (We formed the chamfers using a table-mounted router and chamfer bit.) Sand the base smooth.

6. Glue and clamp the uprights into dadoes, checking that they are square with the base. Remove excess glue with a damp cloth.

7. Cut a piece of 1/16" cork to 3⁵/₁₆X8". Glue the cork to the bottom of the base (we used wood-worker's glue). The cork sits in ⅛" in from each edge. Cut and glue a piece of cork between the uprights.

The shakers come next

1. From ½" stock, rip and crosscut one strip 1¾" wide by 30½" long. Cut three 10"-long pieces from the strip. Now, glue and clamp the pieces together face to face with the

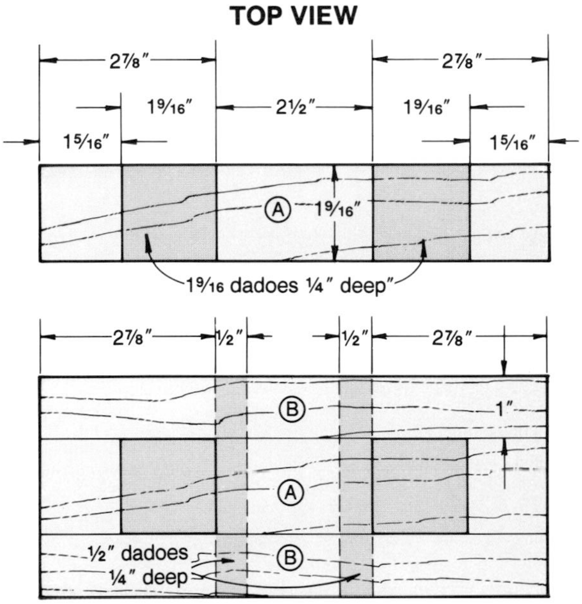
TOP VIEW
2⅞"
2⅞"
1⁹⁄₁₆"
2½"
1⁹⁄₁₆"
1⁵⁄₁₆"
1⁵⁄₁₆"
A
1⁹⁄₁₆"
1⁹⁄₁₆ dadoes ¼" deep
2⅞"
½"
½"
2⅞"
B
1"
A
½" dadoes
¼" deep
B

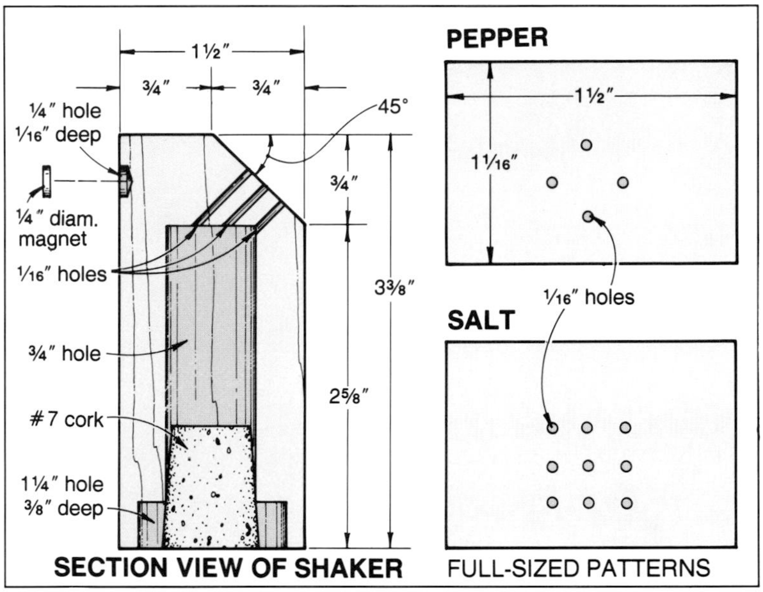
1½"
¾"
¾"
¼" hole
¹⁄₁₆" deep
45°
¾"
¼" diam.
magnet
¹⁄₁₆" holes
3⅜"
¾" hole
2⅝"
#7 cork
1¼" hole
⅜" deep
SECTION VIEW OF SHAKER
PEPPER
1½"
1¹⁄₁₆"
¹⁄₁₆" holes
SALT
FULL-SIZED PATTERNS

edges and ends flush. (You'll need a lamination this long for safe machining in the next step.)

2. Remove the clamps and scrape the excess glue. Rip or joint the edges (not the faces) for a 1½"-square lamination.

3. Crosscut both ends of the 10"-long lamination square. Now, measure 3⅜" in from each end and mark cutoff lines across the lamination. Repeat for the other end. Then, using a combination square and the dimensions on the Shaker Section View drawing *above right*, mark an angled cutline on each end of the lamination.

4. Cut each of the two shakers to 3⅜" length; *do not* angle-cut the pieces yet.

5. Mark diagonals on the bottom end of each shaker to find center.

With a Forstner bit, bore a 1¼" hole ⅜" deep centered into the bottom of each shaker. Switch to a ¾" Forstner bit, and bore a 2⅝"-deep hole centered inside the 1¼" hole. See the Section View drawing for reference.

6. Angle-cut the top end of each shaker (we used our radial-arm saw to make the angled cut).

7. Push a #7 cork into the ¾" hole in each shaker. If the bottom of the cork protrudes, belt-sand the cork flush with the shaker bottom.

Drill the holes and add the magnets and finish

1. Trace or photocopy the full-sized hole and outline patterns *above* onto white paper. Cut the outlines to shape and adhere one to the angled surface of each shaker with spray-on adhesive or double-faced tape.

2. Clamp a shaker into a vise with the angled surface level. Make an indentation at each hole mark with an awl. This keeps the drill bit from wandering when drilling the holes. Then, drill ¹⁄₁₆" holes where indented. Remove the pattern and repeat with the second shaker.

3. Sand the base and shakers smooth. Stain if desired (we left ours natural) and apply the finish.

4. To remove any finish that may have seeped into the ¹⁄₁₆" condiment holes, hold a ¹⁄₁₆" drill bit with your fingers. Then, insert the bit into each hole, and twist the bit with your fingers.

5. Drill a ¼" hole ¹⁄₁₆" deep in each upright where located on the Base drawing *opposite*. Place a ¼" dowel center in each hole. Position a shaker in each dadoed recess and press each against the dowel center to transfer the mating magnet hole location to the shaker. Drill a ¼" hole ¹⁄₁₆" deep into each shaker where indented.

6. With instant glue or epoxy, glue a magnet in each hole. Check that each magnet faces the right way to attract the mating magnet.

Project Tool List

Tablesaw
  Dado blade or dado set
Radial arm saw
Portable drill
Drill press
  Bits: ¹⁄₁₆", ¼", ¾", 1¼"
Router
  Router table
  Chamfer bit
Finishing sander

Note: *We built the project using the tools listed. You may be able to substitute other tools or equipment for listed items you don't have. Additional common hand tools and clamps may be required to complete the project.*

Bill of Materials

Part	Finished Size*			Mat.	Qty.
	T	W	L		
A base center	½"	1⁹⁄₁₆"	8¼"	O	1
B base edges	½"	1"	8¼"	O	2
C uprights	½"	3⁹⁄₁₆"	4¼"	O	2
D* shakers	1½"	1½"	3⅜"	LO	2

*Part marked with an * is laminated oversize and then trimmed to size. Please read the instructions before cutting.

Material Key: O—oak, LO—laminated oak.
Supplies: two #7 corks, spray-on adhesive or double-faced tape, finish, ¹⁄₁₆"-thick cork, four ¼"-diameter magnets.

NO-PROBLEM PIZZA PADDLE

You'll be a snack-time hero after you make this great pizza handler. No more sizzled fingertips from hauling the pizza out of the oven! No more scars on the cookware from the pizza cutter! No more pieces hanging over the edge of a too-small serving plate! From oven to table, this server makes pizza fun.

Note: We used ½"-thick maple for this project. You can plane or resaw thicker stock.

1. Rip and crosscut three boards to ½x4½x24". You'll edge-glue them together, so here's a procedure that helps control cupping by alternating the grain. It also ensures a flat glue-up by compensating for minor deviations from 90° in your tablesaw setup.

•Rip all three boards with the arcs in the end grain pointing up. Saw both edges on one board.

•Flip this piece over, and place it between the two remaining pieces, as shown in the Gluing Up the Stock drawing, *opposite*.

•Apply woodworker's glue (we used Titebond II water-resistant glue), and clamp.

2. Now, draw a centerline lengthwise on the back of the edge-joined stock. Mark a centerpoint 7" in from one end on that line, and draw a 13"-diameter circle (using a 6½" radius). Then, trace the full-sized handle pattern *opposite, bottom,* onto the board, aligning it along the centerline and joining the circle to create a giant paddle. Cut out the paddle with your scrollsaw or bandsaw, staying slightly outside the pattern line.

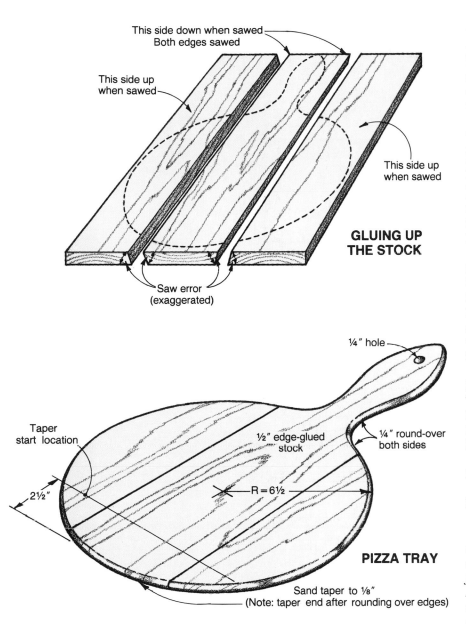

This side down when sawed
Both edges sawed

This side up when sawed

This side up when sawed

GLUING UP THE STOCK

Saw error (exaggerated)

3. Sand to the line, and rout a ¼" round-over around the paddle's perimeter on both sides. Drill a ¼" hole where shown. Draw a line across the paddle that's perpendicular to the centerline, 2½" from the rounded end.

4. Clamp the paddle to your workbench, with the pencil line facing up and the rounded end jutting past the edge. With your portable belt sander, start from the line and taper-sand the server to ⅛" thick at the front edge. (We made fast work of this operation with 24- and 36-grit belts.)

5. Sand out the grit marks from the coarse belts with progressively finer belts to 120-grit. Turn to your finishing sander for final smoothing. Finally, apply a food-safe coating such as Behlen's Salad Bowl Finish while you figure out the guest list for your pizza party.

Project Tool List
Tablesaw
Bandsaw
Portable belt sander
Router
  ¼" round-over bit
Portable drill
  ¼" bit
Finishing sander

Note: We built the project using the tools listed. You may be able to substitute other tools or equipment for listed items you don't have. Additional common hand tools and clamps may be required to complete the project.

¼" hole

Taper start location

2½"

½" edge-glued stock

¼" round-over both sides

R = 6½

PIZZA TRAY

Sand taper to ⅛"
(Note: taper end after rounding over edges)

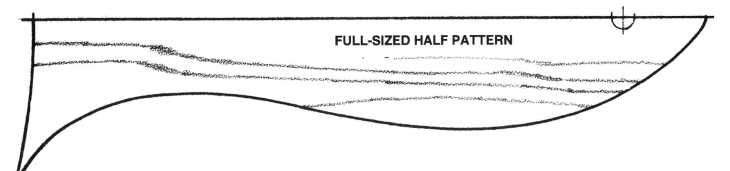

FULL-SIZED HALF PATTERN

GET A HANDLE ON THESE SHARP STEAK KNIVES

What's almost as good as a really tender steak? You guessed it—a really sharp knife for cutting it! We teamed up with master knifemaker Walt Easley for this great design. You can make a set of these great knives in an evening. And after you do, you'll never have to say uncle to a tough steak again.

Note: You'll need ³⁄₁₆"-thick stock for the knife handles. (We resawed a 1½" teak turning square.) See the Buying Guide, opposite, for our sources for the knife blades and handle stock.

1. Before you do anything else, tape the cardboard protective sleeve to each blade for safe handling. (The carbon-vanadium alloy blades are *sharp*.) Fasten the sleeve with masking tape, wrapping it onto the knife tang, ¼" behind the heel of the blade (shown on the Exploded View drawing, *opposite*).

2. Lay the tape straight across the tang because you'll align the ends of the handle pieces with it later. Stick some tape over the open end of the sleeve, too.

3. Rip ³⁄₁₆"-thick stock to 1" wide, and then crosscut a 4" length for each handle side. Cut 12 pieces for the set of six knives. Refer to the Sanding Chamfers drawing *opposite,* and sand a 20° chamfer on one end of each piece, leaving a ¹⁄₁₆" square end. Copy the guide angle from the drawing.

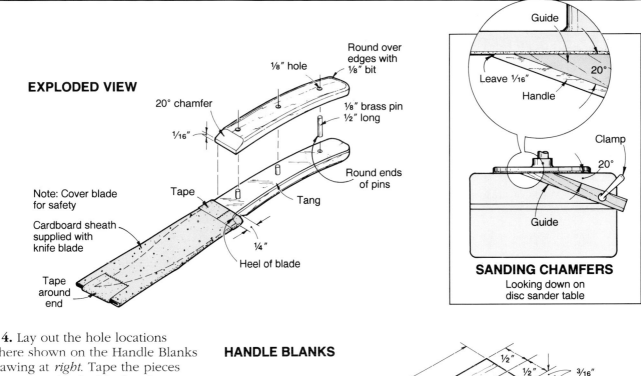

EXPLODED VIEW

1/8" hole

20° chamfer

Round over edges with 1/8" bit

1/16"

1/8" brass pin 1/2" long

Note: Cover blade for safety

Tape

Round ends of pins

Cardboard sheath supplied with knife blade

Tang

1/4"

Heel of blade

Tape around end

SANDING CHAMFERS

Guide

Leave 1/16"

20°

Handle

Clamp

20°

Guide

Looking down on disc sander table

4. Lay out the hole locations where shown on the Handle Blanks drawing at *right*. Tape the pieces into pairs with double-faced tape, and then drill 1/8" holes where marked with a brad-point bit in a drill press. Hold the handle blanks with a handscrew clamp. (We backed them with scrap to prevent tear-out.)

5. Slightly round the ends of the provided 1/8" brass pins with sandpaper to prevent tearout when you push them through the handle holes. Roughen the sides of the knife tang with coarse sandpaper. If you're putting on teak handles, as we did, remove the oil from the mating surfaces of the teak with acetone. Don't touch the surfaces after cleaning.

6. Glue the handle sides to the tang with slow-set epoxy. Align the holes in the handle sides with the tang holes, and then tap the brass pins into place. Butt the handle pieces up to the tape on the tang, and then clamp.

7. After the epoxy sets, file the brass pins down to the handle surface. Sand the handle edges flush with the knife tang, using a belt sander. Round over the edges with a piloted 1/8" round-over bit in

HANDLE BLANKS

Sand handle ends to chamfer indicated by dotted lines

4"

1/2"

1/2"

3/16"

1 5/16"

1 5/16"

1/2"

1/2"

9/16"

a table-mounted router or with 80-grit sandpaper.

8. Finish-sand the handles, and apply three coats of a clear oil finish, such as tung oil. Remove the blade sheaths, and then grill up some steak. When it's time to do the dishes, wipe the handles with a damp cloth, submersing only the blades—the finish will last longer that way.

Buying Guide

• **Blades.** Set of six knife blades with lifetime guarantee and 1/8" brass handle pins. For current prices, contact Easley Knives, P.O. Box 478, Gladbrook, IA 50635, or call 515-473-3182.

• **Handles.** Teak turning square, 1½x1½x18". For current prices,

contact Constantine's, 2050 Eastchester Rd., Bronx, NY 10461, or call 800-223-8087.

Project Tool List
Tablesaw
Disc sander
Belt sander
Drill press
  1/8" bit
Router
  Router table
  1/8" round-over bit

Note: *We built the project using the tools listed. You may be able to substitute other tools or equipment for listed items you don't have. Additional common hand tools and clamps may be required to complete the project.*

WELL-ORDERED CUTLERY CASE

The Walt Easley steak knives featured on *pages 82–83* make the perfect gift for so many occasions that we decided to build a fitting presentation box for them. In addition to its practical slotted interior for safe storage, our walnut box also features a slick sliding lid for easy access to those great knives.

Note: *We built the knife box from ¾", ½", and ⅜" walnut. Plane or resaw thicker stock for the ½" and ⅜" material.*

1. Rip and crosscut a piece of ⅜"-thick walnut to 2x36". With a ¼" spiral mortise bit or straight bit in your table-mounted router, cut a groove ¼" deep ¼" from one edge on one side of the stock.

2. Cut two pieces 9¼" long from the grooved stock for the box sides (A). Rip the remainder of the piece to 1½" wide, cutting off the edge opposite the groove. Cut two 4¾" lengths from the piece for the box ends (B).

3. Cut the box bottom (C) to ⅜x4¾x8⅞", and then adjust the table-mounted router to cut a ¼" rabbet ⅛" deep across each end. Make a test cut first to ensure that the rabbet fits the part B grooves.

4. Dry-assemble the ends (B) to the bottom (C), with the rabbeted side down (see the Exploded View drawing *opposite*). Glue on the sides (A), with the groove to the top and inside, applying woodworker's glue to the edges of the ends and bottom. Make sure that the ends are square to the base.

Bill of Materials					
Part	Finished Size			Mat.	Qty.
	T	W	L		
A sides	⅜"	2"	9¼"	W	2
B ends	⅜"	1½"	4¾"	W	2
C bottom	⅜"	4¾"	8⅞"	W	1
D lid	½"	5 3/16"	9¼"	W	1
E spacers	¾"	15/16"	4⅛"	W	2
F spacers	½"	15/16"	4⅛"	W	5
G blade stop	½"	15/16"	4¾"	W	1
H lid stop	1/16"	½"	4½"	W	1
Material Key: W—walnut					

5. Cut ½"-thick stock to 5 3/16x9¼" for the box lid (D). Rout a ¼" rabbet ¼" deep along both top edges of the lid. Slide the lid into the grooves on the sides, and then sand all outside surfaces flush.

6. Change the router bit to a ¼" round-over bit, and rout along the top edges of the box with the lid in place. Sand smooth, and then remove the lid.

7. Cut parts E, F, G, and H to the sizes shown on the Bill of Materials. Glue part G into position. With a disc or belt sander, sand a round-over on one corner of each part E and F. Cut the 9/16" radius where shown with a bandsaw or scrollsaw, and then sand smooth with a 1"-diameter drum sander in a drill press.

8. Cut six ⅛x1x6" spacers from scrapwood. Now, glue a part E at one side of the box with the round cutout at the end nearest part G. Next, place a ⅛" spacer *but do not glue it in,* and then glue in a part F. Continue adding spacers and part F blocks, ending with the remaining part E. Sand part E to fit, if necessary.

9. Finish as desired. (We used Watco Dark Walnut Stain followed by three coats of natural Watco Danish Oil Finish.)

10. To apply the lid stop (H), sand an area on the underside of the lid where shown on the Gluing the Lid Stop drawing *opposite, bottom.* Slide the lid into place, leaving it partially open so you can reach the sanded area. Apply a small amount of epoxy to the stop and, with the box upside down, center the stop about ¼" from the inside edge of the lid. Now, gently slide the lid closed to push the stop into position. Make sure that the lid is flush, and let the epoxy cure.

Project Tool List

Tablesaw
Bandsaw or scrollsaw
Disc or belt sander
Drill press
  1" drum sander
Router
  Router table
  Bits: ¼" straight, ¼" rabbet
Finishing sander

Note: *We built the project using the tools listed. You may be able to substitute other tools or equipment for listed items you don't have. Additional common hand tools and clamps may be required to complete the project.*

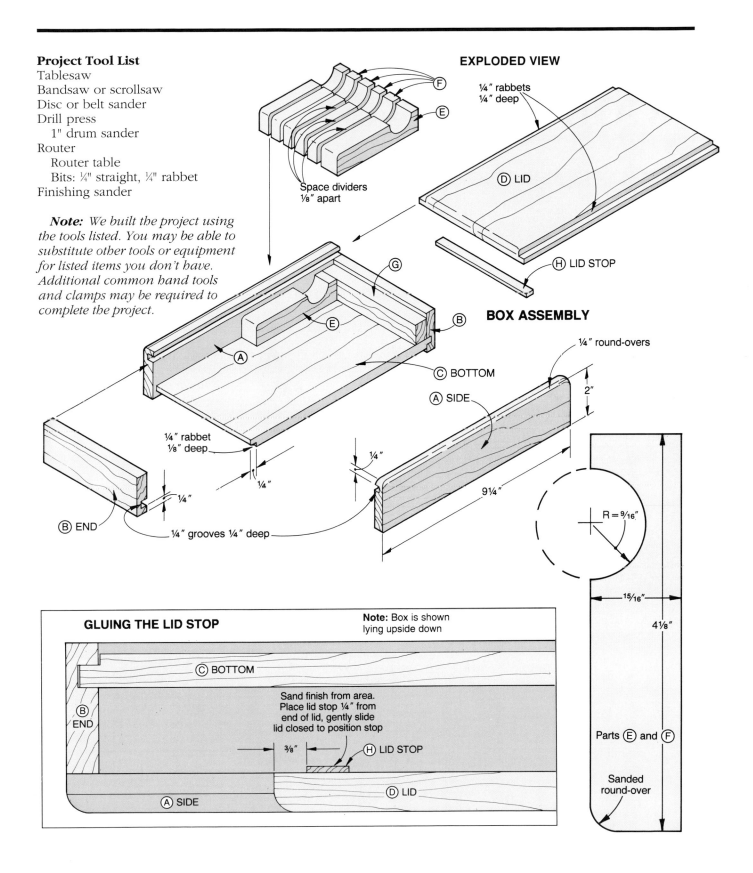

EXPLODED VIEW

¼" rabbets
¼" deep

Ⓓ LID

Ⓗ LID STOP

Space dividers ⅛" apart

Ⓕ
Ⓔ

Ⓖ

Ⓔ

Ⓐ

Ⓑ

Ⓒ BOTTOM

BOX ASSEMBLY

¼" round-overs

2"

Ⓐ SIDE

9¼"

¼" rabbet ⅛" deep

¼"

¼"

¼"

Ⓑ END

¼" grooves ¼" deep

R = ⁹⁄₁₆"

¹⁵⁄₁₆"

4⅛"

Parts Ⓔ and Ⓕ

Sanded round-over

GLUING THE LID STOP

Note: Box is shown lying upside down

Ⓒ BOTTOM

Ⓑ END

Sand finish from area. Place lid stop ¼" from end of lid, gently slide lid closed to position stop

⅜"

Ⓗ LID STOP

Ⓐ SIDE

Ⓓ LID

STRAIGHT 'N' NARROW NOODLE CUTTER

Give your favorite gourmet cook the "cutting edge" with this unusual hand-turned gadget.

Note: Turning the noodle cutter's coves and cutting edges requires careful, consistent tool control. Practice those cuts on scrap material before beginning the project.

First things first

1. Mount a 3×3×18" turning square between centers, and round it down to 2¾" diameter with the ⅜" or ½" gouge. Gauge the diameter at the ends and several points along the length with outside calipers.

2. Lay out the turning on your rounded blank with a sharp pencil. Starting at the headstock end, leave ⅝" for waste. From there, mark consecutively a 2" section for the ball end of the handle, 1" for the handle cone, 11" for the main coved body, another 1" handle cone, and another 2" ball end. The remaining portion at the tailstock end will be waste. (See full-sized half pattern *opposite* for reference.)

3. With the ⅛" parting tool, cut ⅜" deep on the outside and inside of each ball end, leaving a full 2" width for the ball. Next, taper the areas from each end of the 11" center section toward the ball. Now, turn the center section to 2⅝" diameter. Check the surface for unevenness with a steel straightedge, and gauge the diameter at the ends with calipers to insure that the cylinder is true.

4. Sand the center section with 150-grit sandpaper, and then recheck with the straightedge. Complete the sanding with 220-grit and then 400-grit sandpaper.

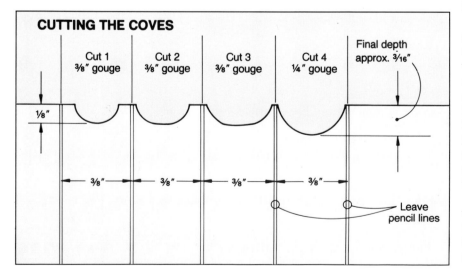

CUTTING THE COVES

| Cut 1
⅜" gouge | Cut 2
⅜" gouge | Cut 3
⅜" gouge | Cut 4
¼" gouge | Final depth
approx. ³⁄₁₆" |

⅛"

⅜" ⅜" ⅜" ⅜"

Leave pencil lines

Now for the cutting edges

1. Transfer the template from the full-sized half pattern at *right* to posterboard, and cut it out with an X-acto knife. Now, on your turning, lay out marks ⅜" on center along the 11" section, starting from the middle and working toward each end. With the lathe at a slow speed, about 800 rpm, draw a pencil line around the cylinder at each mark. These will be the noodle-cutting edges. (See the half pattern for reference.)

2. Now, refer to the Cutting the Coves drawing *opposite, bottom,* and cut ⅛" deep midway between each pair of lines with the ⅜" gouge. Next, widen each cove with two careful cuts, one from the pencil line on each side to the center of the cove. Start each cut *at* the pencil line, but be sure to leave the line.

3. Then, with a ¼" gouge and working from one end of the noodle cutter to the other, round out the coves to about 3⁄16" deep.

4. Maintain the symmetry and consistent shape of the coves by checking with the template.

5. With the lathe running, sand inside the coves with 150-grit sandpaper rolled into a tube. Follow with 220-grit. With the lathe stopped, lightly sand the cutting edges—just enough to erase the pencil lines—with 400-grit sandpaper. Be sure the cutters don't come to a knife edge.

Here's how to turn the ball handles

1. Part in to 2" diameter in the middle of each ball section, checking with calipers. Remove the waste on either side almost to the parting-cut depth. Cut in to about 1" deep on each side of each ball section. Now, form the ball ends with the ⅜" gouge. Make room for the tool by cutting into the handle cone area and the waste areas on the ends of the turning.

2. Part in to ⅝" diameter at the point where the ball joins the cone, checking with calipers as you cut in. Sand the ball ends and cones with 150-grit sandpaper followed by 220-grit.

3. Cut the waste ends to ⅛" diameter. Shut off the lathe, and remove the turning with a coping saw. Sand the area to match the ball contour in graduating grits up to 400-grit sandpaper.

4. Finish the noodle cutter with a food-safe finish such as Behlen's Salad Bowl Finish.

Supplies

3x3x18" turning square of hard maple, yellow birch, or other close-grained hardwood; centers; outside calipers; tape measure; straightedge.

Project Tool List

Lathe
- Spur drive center
- Tail center
- ¼", ⅜", ½" gouges
- ⅛" parting tool

Note: *We built the project using the tools listed. You may be able to substitute other tools or equipment for listed items you don't have. Additional common hand tools and clamps may be required to complete the project.*

Lathe Speeds

Roughing: 500–800 rpm
Finish Cutting: 800–1200 rpm
Sanding: 1200–2000 rpm

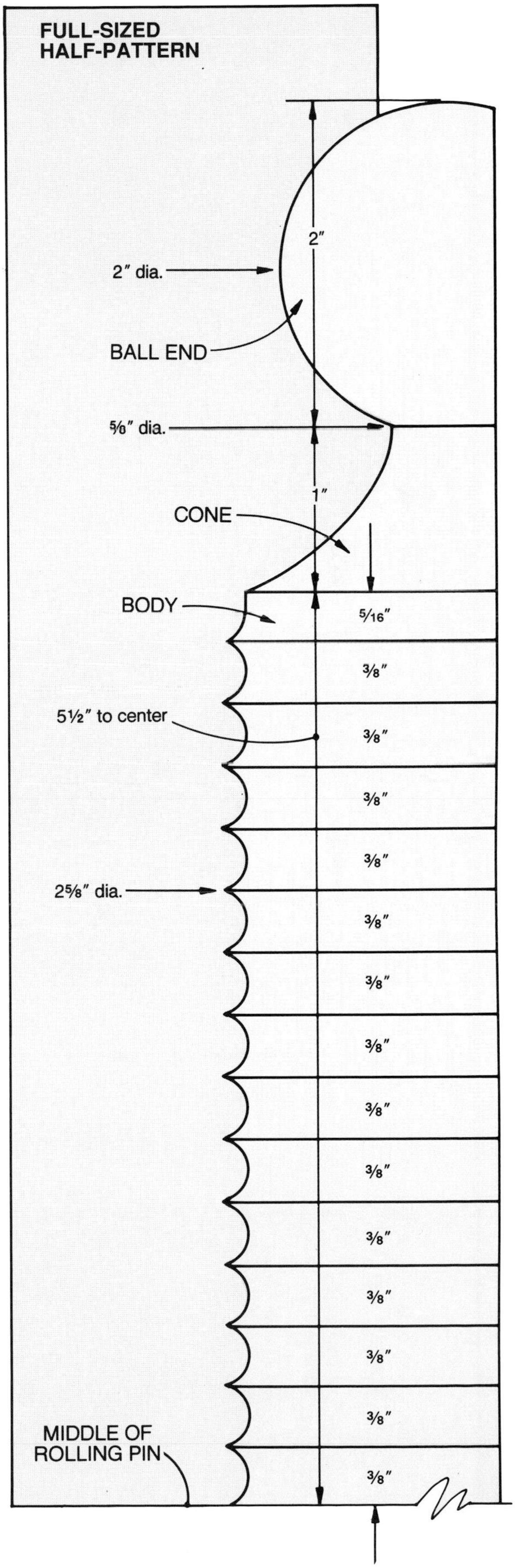
FULL-SIZED
HALF-PATTERN
2"
2" dia.
BALL END
⅝" dia.
1"
CONE
BODY
5⁄16"
⅜"
5½" to center
⅜"
⅜"
⅜"
2⅝" dia.
⅜"
⅜"
⅜"
⅜"
⅜"
⅜"
⅜"
⅜"
⅜"
MIDDLE OF
ROLLING PIN
⅜"

WALNUT-CLAD PUMP DISPENSER

Here's a handy pump dispenser for soap or hand lotion that's easy to build and looks great, too. Your reward for a little effort on this one: the perfect finishing touch for your kitchen or bathroom.

Note: You'll need ¼"-thick stock for this project (we used walnut). Plane thicker stock to size, or resaw the stock.

1. From ¼"-thick stock, cut two 2⅞" squares for the top and bottom, then bevel-rip eight pieces 1⅛x5⅛" at 22½° for the sides.

2. Lay the sides, bevel down, next to each other on your workbench. Align the ends and tape the pieces together with masking tape or reinforced strapping tape. (See the Body Strips drawing *opposite*.) Turn the assembly over, and roll it into an octagon, checking all joints for a tight fit.

3. Unroll the sides, then apply woodworker's glue to the open joints. Roll up the sides again, making sure all joints are tight. Secure with tape until the glue sets.

4. Use a Forstner bit or holesaw to bore a 1⅛" hole in the center of one square. Back it with scrapwood to prevent tear-out. Then, using the body as a guide, cut the corners off both squares, leaving a margin on all sides.

5. Remove the pump assembly from the bottle, and slide the bottle into the body. Now, glue the top into place, locating the hole in the top over the bottle neck.

6. With a disc or belt sander, sand the edges of the top flush with the body sides. Then, sand 45° chamfers on the top edges. (We used a miter gauge for accuracy, but a guide block clamped to the sander table also would work.)

7. With the bottom held firmly to the body, mark and drill four ¹⁄₁₆" holes ⅝" deep through the bottom and into the body's sides. Enlarge the holes in the bottom to ³⁄₃₂", and then countersink them.

8. Attach the bottom with four #2×½" flathead brass wood screws. Sand the bottom edges flush with the sides, and then remove the bottom. To keep the bottle from turning inside the body, glue it to the bottom with hotmelt adhesive.

9. Apply a clear, durable finish (we used a wipe-on polyurethane product), and then install the bottom. Now, you're ready to fill the dispenser and pump your hand lotion in style.

Buying Guide
•Bottle and dispenser.
Plastic bottle with screw-on pump-type dispenser. For current prices, contact Ennis Mountain Woods, RFD 2, Box 222B, Afton, VA 22920, or call 703-456-8215 after 5 p.m. EST.

Project Tool List
Tablesaw
Disc or belt sander
Portable drill
Drill press
  Bits: ¹⁄₁₆", ³⁄₃₂", 1⅛"
Finishing sander

Note: We built the project using the tools listed. You may be able to substitute other tools or equipment for listed items you don't have. Additional common hand tools and clamps may be required to complete the project.

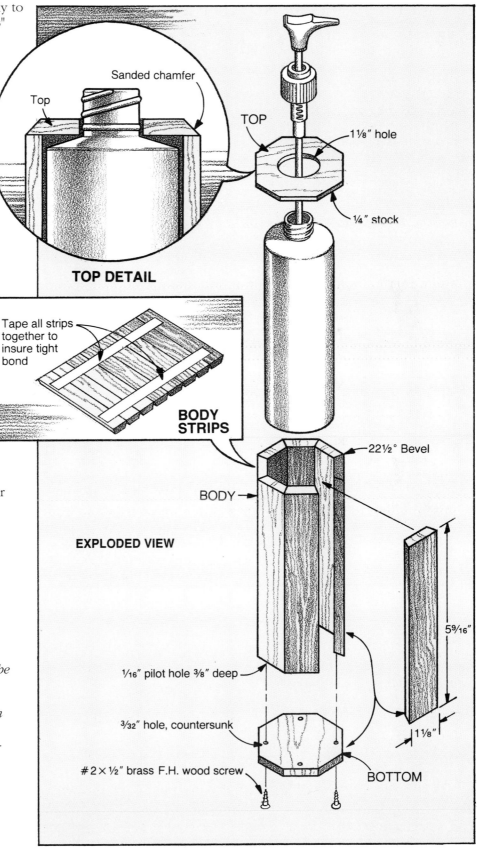

Top

Sanded chamfer

Top

TOP DETAIL

Tape all strips together to insure tight bond

BODY STRIPS

TOP

1⅛" hole

¼" stock

22½° Bevel

BODY

EXPLODED VIEW

¹⁄₁₆" pilot hole ⅜" deep

5⁹⁄₁₆"

1⅛"

³⁄₃₂" hole, countersunk

#2 × ½" brass F.H. wood screw

BOTTOM

SUNBURST SINK BOARD

I n our travels around the
country, we see thousands of
handcrafted cutting boards. But
this one-of-a-kind design
originated right here in our
shop. Jim Boelling, our project
builder, made these as gifts
years ago. Jim's shortcuts make
cutting and laminating the
maple and walnut strips a snap
for a stunning finished product.

*Note: This cutting board was
made to fit a standard sink with a
basin interior measuring 14 x 15¾".
For a smaller sink, construct the
laminated board as described, and
cut it to size later. If your sink is
larger, you'll need to make longer
laminations and change the cutting
angle of the taper jig.*

First, cut and laminate the maple and walnut

1. Rip and crosscut seven pieces
of 1¹⁄₁₆" -thick maple (five-quarter
stock) to 2¾" wide by 22½" long for
parts A. (We cut all seven pieces
from a board 6" wide by 8' long.)

2. For the walnut strips (B), set
your table saw fence ¼" away from
the inside edge of the saw blade.
Rip 14 strips ¼" wide from the edge
of a piece of 1¹⁄₁₆"-thick walnut 22½"

long. You also could cut 7 pieces
of ¾" stock to 1¹⁄₁₆" wide by 22½"
long, and then resaw two ¼" strips
from each piece.

3. With the surfaces flush, glue
and clamp two walnut strips (one
along each edge) to each piece
of maple. Later, scrape off the
excess glue.

Make the taper jig and cut the wedges

1. Cut a piece of ¾" plywood
to 6" wide by 30" long. Mark
three reference points where
dimensioned on the Taper Jig
drawing *opposite, left*. Using a
framing square, draw two lines to
connect the points.

2. Cut along the marked lines to
form the wedge-shaped taper in the
plywood (we used a bandsaw).

3. Position your table saw fence
and jig where shown on the Cutting
the Wedges drawing *opposite, right*.
Now, using the drawing as a guide,
cut *two* wedge-shaped pieces from
each lamination.

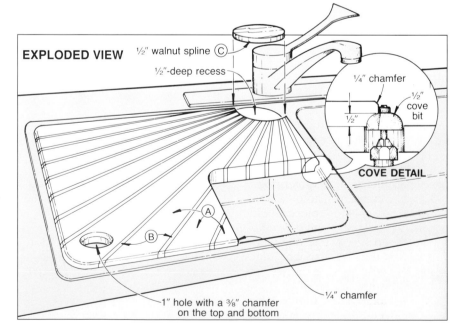

EXPLODED VIEW
½" walnut spline Ⓒ
½"-deep recess
¼" chamfer
½" cove bit
½"
COVE DETAIL
1" hole with a ⅜" chamfer
on the top and bottom
¼" chamfer

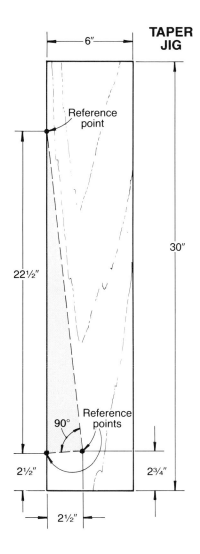

TAPER JIG

6"

Reference point

30"

22½"

90° Reference points

2½"

2¾"

2½"

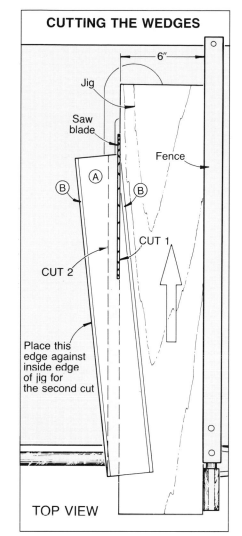

CUTTING THE WEDGES

6"

Jig

Saw blade

Fence

Ⓐ

Ⓑ   Ⓑ

CUT 1

CUT 2

Place this edge against inside edge of jig for the second cut

TOP VIEW

Tap the wedges into the corner of the clamping jig, and then hold the wedges in position with nails.

Here's how to laminate the wedges

1. To form the clamping jig shown in the photo at *right*, lay a piece of plywood about 30" square on top of your workbench. Now, cut two pieces of ¾"-thick scrap stock about 1" wide by 26" long. Nail one of the strips onto the plywood near an edge. Then, position the 14 wedges, edge to edge, with the points converging where shown in the photo. While holding the laminated pieces tightly against one another, nail the second scrap strip to the plywood and against the other straight edge of the wedges. Remove the wedges from the clamping jig.

2. Lay waxed paper on the plywood between the strips. Spread woodworker's glue on the mating edges of the wedges, and position them where shown in the photo *above*. Now, lightly tap the pieces toward the inside corner of the jig, and drive a #6 finish nail into position at the end of each wedge. Check for a flush top surface and

tight joints. (We found it necessary to tap a few of the wedges in tighter and renail after initially nailing all the wedges in place.)

3. Let the glue dry, remove the nails, and scrape the excess glue from the lamination.

Cut the template and cutting board to shape

1. Measure the interior opening (front to back and side to side) of your sink basin (we measured ours 1" from the top edge). On a piece of cardboard, mark layout lines the exact size of your basin opening.

2. Mark a radius at three of the corners to connect the layout lines on the cardboard. Leave a square corner where the walnut strips converge; you'll mark and cut it to shape later. (To determine the necessary radius for a tight fit onto the sink basin later, we marked different-sized radii on cardboard scraps, and cut them to shape. Next, we trial-fit each scrap against the rounded inside corner of the sink. Once we found the right radius, it became a template to mark the three radii onto the cardboard template.)

3. Draw four more lines ⅜" *outside* and *parallel* to the first lines drawn (later these will be the outside edges of the cutting board). Connect the *outside* lines by marking radii ⅜" larger than the ones marked in the previous step (our outside radii measured 2⅝"). Carefully cut the cardboard template to shape.

4. Mark the location, draw the 1" finger hole circle, and cut the hole in the template to shape.

5. Position the cardboard template on the sink board lamination and trace its outline and the finger hole location onto the sink board. (You may need to move the finger hole around a bit until it is centered over a piece of maple.)

6. Position the rip fence on your table saw (we moved ours 16½" away from the inside edge of the blade), and trim the board where shown on the drawing on *page 92*. Next, cut the other two edges

continued

SUNBURST SINK BOARD

continued

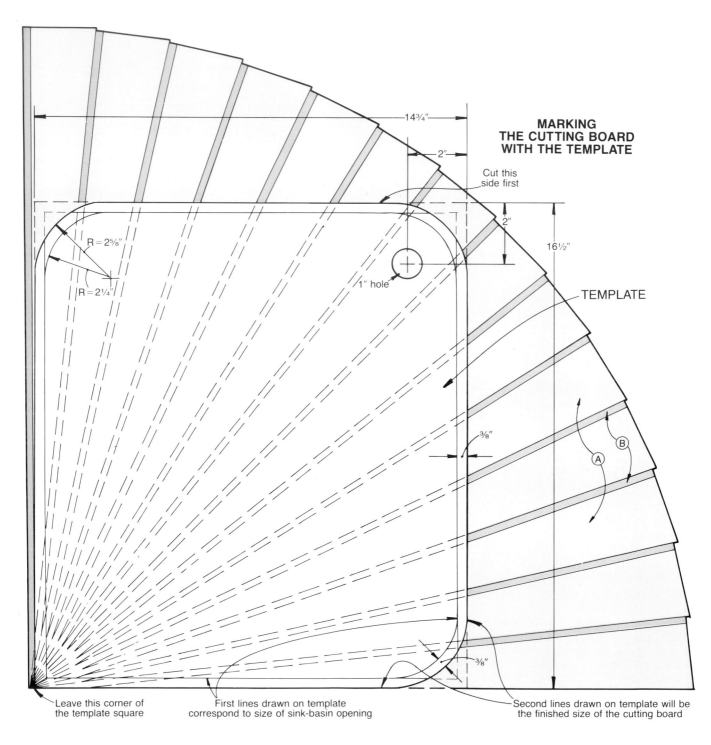

**MARKING
THE CUTTING BOARD
WITH THE TEMPLATE**

14¾"

2"

Cut this
side first

2"

1" hole

16½"

TEMPLATE

R = 2⅝"

R = 2¼"

⅜"

A   B

⅜"

Leave this corner of
the template square

First lines drawn on template
correspond to size of sink-basin opening

Second lines drawn on template will be
the finished size of the cutting board

square. Finally, use a bandsaw to cut the three rounded corners, and then sand them smooth.

7. Bore a 1" finger hole through the cutting board where marked.

Now for the surface spline

1. Cut a piece of 1¼₆" stock to 8" square for the drilling jig. Mark diagonals to find center.

2. Mark and cut a 3⅝"-square notch at one corner of the jig where shown on the drawing *opposite, top.*

3. Chuck a circle cutter to your drill press, and position the *outside edge* of the cutter blade 3¼" from the center of the pilot bit. Raise the bottom tip of the cutter ¼" higher than the bottom of the bit. For a cleaner cut, you want the bit to make contact with the jig before the cutter enters the lamination.

4. Center the jig under the pilot bit, and clamp it to the drill press table. Slide the cutting board into the notched corner, and clamp it to the table. Start the drill, and *slowly* cut into the jig and sink board until you've cut ½" deep with the cutter. Remove the cutting board and jig from the drill press table.

5. Fit your router with a ½" straight bit. Clamp the sink board and drilling jig (the jig helps support the router) to a workbench. Starting at the outside edges and working in, rout a ½"-deep recess in the corner of the board. Rout just up to the groove you cut with the circle cutter. Now, as shown in the photo at *right,* clean the ridge between the routed area and circle-cutter groove with a ½" chisel.

6. Mark a 3¼" radius on a piece of ½" walnut where shown on the drawing *below.* Cutting just outside the line, bandsaw the surface spline (C) to shape. Check the fit of the spline into the routed recess, and sand if necessary.

7. Glue and clamp the walnut spline into the recess, noting the direction of grain shown on the Exploded View drawing on *page*

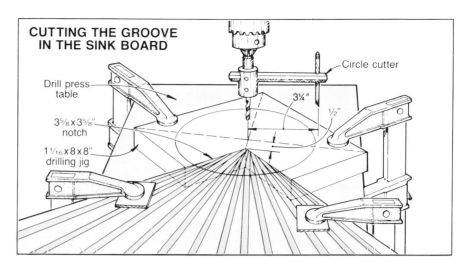

After routing the excess material, clean the surface between the routed area and circle-cutter groove with a sharp chisel.

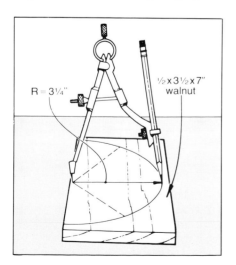

90. After the glue dries, use the cardboard template to mark the radius on the splined corner, and cut it to shape.

Sanding, routing, and finishing

1. Sand the sink board smooth.

2. Rout a ½" cove along the bottom edge of the sink board (see the Cove detail accompanying the Exploded View drawing).

3. Rout a ¼" chamfer along the top edge of the sink board and ⅜" chamfers on both edges of the 1" finger hole.

4. Finish-sand the sink board, and apply the finish (we used Behlen's Salad Bowl Finish).

Project Tool List
Tablesaw
Bandsaw
Drill press
   Circle cutter
   1" bit
Router
   Bits: ½" straight, ½" cove, chamfer
Finishing sander

Note: We built the project using the tools listed. You may be able to substitute other tools or equipment for listed items you don't have. Additional common hand tools and clamps may be required to complete the project.

HOT-STUFF OAK SERVER

4. With the pieces still taped together, drill the four ⅜" holes. Back the pieces with scrap to prevent chip-out. With that done, separate and finish-sand the two ends.

Just think how impressed your guests will be when you present a scrumptious, piping-hot casserole or other tasty treat in this winning server. And you'll be equally impressed when you discover how easily this project goes together. We made several of them as gifts recently—in almost no time at all.

Note: We designed our server to accept a 13x9x2" (33x23x5 cm) Pyrex baking dish. But you could just as easily tailor it to accommodate other sizes.

Shape the ends first

1. Cut a pair of hardwood scraps (we used oak) to 3 x 11" long. Using double-faced tape, stick them together.

2. Using carbon paper, transfer the full-size pattern for the ends (A) shown *opposite,* and the dowel-hole centerpoints, onto one of the pieces. Then, with your bandsaw, cut the pieces to shape.

3. Sand to the pattern line with a disc and/or drum sander. (We used a ¾" drum sander and a setup like the one shown *above right* to sand up to the lines in the notched areas.)

Bill of Materials				
Part	Finished Size*		Mat.	Qty.
	T	W	L		
A* ends	¾"	2⅜"	10½"	O	2
B handles	1" dia.		11"	O	2
C top rails	⅜" dia.		15"	O	2
D btm. rails	⅜" dia.		18"	O	2

*Part marked with an * is cut larger initially, then trimmed to finished size. Please read the instructions before cutting.

Material Key: O—oak

EXPLODED VIEW

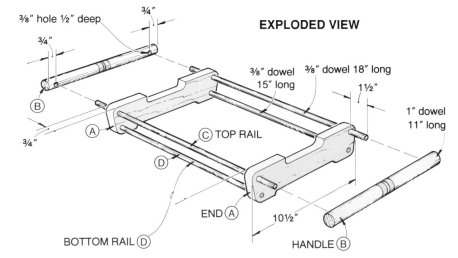

⅜" hole ½" deep
¾"
¾"
¾"
⅜" dowel 15" long
⅜" dowel 18" long
1½"
1" dowel 11" long
Ⓑ
Ⓐ
Ⓒ TOP RAIL
Ⓓ
END Ⓐ
10½"
BOTTOM RAIL Ⓓ
HANDLE Ⓑ

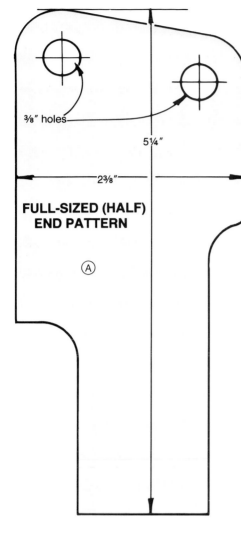

⅜" holes

5¼"

2⅜"

**FULL-SIZED (HALF)
END PATTERN**

Ⓐ

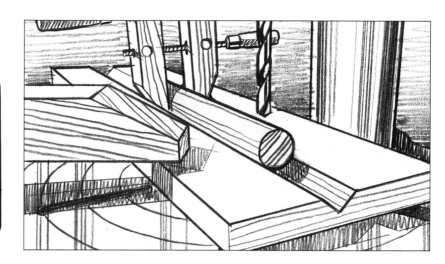

Now for the rails and handles

Note: If you prefer to make the more decorative laminated handles for your server, follow the 4-step sequence that follows under "Alternate handles," then go to step 2.

1. From a 1" dowel, cut two 11" lengths for the handles (B).

2. From two lengths of ⅜" dowel, cut two 18"-long pieces and two more 15"-long pieces for the top and bottom side rails (C, D). Set aside your rails for now.

3. To drill the dowel handles for the ⅜" top rails, first cut a V-groove in scrap. Center the V-groove under the drill bit and clamp it in place. Lay a dowel handle in the groove and clamp as shown *above right* to prevent its turning. Drill both handles.

Putting it all together

1. Apply a small amount of glue to the inside of the two bottom holes in each end, and then insert the ⅜" side rails flush with the outside surface. Allow the glue to dry. Sand the dowel ends flush with the end pieces.

2. Push the top rails through the upper holes in the ends so they extend 1½" past the end. (We stopped when the dowels were ¾" beyond the end, applied glue around each dowel on the area about to enter the hole, then drove them the rest of the way.) Next apply glue to the holes in the 1" dowels, and insert the projecting top rail dowels into them. Wipe away glue squeeze-out.

3. Finish the server as desired. (We applied three coats of semigloss clear lacquer, sanding between coats.)

Alternate handles

1. Using a 1" hole saw and two woods of contrasting thicknesses, cut two sets of three wood discs.

2. Drill ¼" holes 1¹⁄₁₆" deep into the ends of four 1" dowels. (We moved our drill press table aside, laid a 2 x 4 scrap across it but below the chuck, and clamped it. Next, we bored a 1" hole through the 2 x 4. Switching to a ¼" bit, we inserted each dowel in the 2 x 4 and drilled the holes.)

3. Sandwich the thinner, contrasting-color wood discs between the two thicker discs, and center both sets on 3" lengths of ¼" dowel

as shown *below*. Next, glue and clamp the discs together and to the dowel. (We used two small woodscrew clamps.) After the glue dries, test assemble the handles. Shorten the ¼" dowel if necessary to fit.

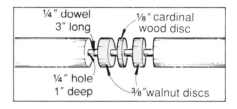

¼" dowel 3" long
⅛" cardinal wood disc
¼" hole 1" deep
⅜" walnut discs

4. Figure the dowel lengths needed for each handle by subtracting the width of the lamination from 11" (or length of your handle) and divide by two. Square dowel ends, then crosscut the four lengths you need, measuring from the drilled ends. Glue and assemble the parts.

Project Tool List
Tablesaw
Bandsaw
Drill press
 ¾" drum sander
 ⅜" bit
 For alternate handles: 1" holesaw;
  ¼", 1" bits
Finishing sander

Note: We built the project using the tools listed. You may be able to substitute other tools or equipment for listed items you don't have. Additional common hand tools and clamps may be required to complete the project.

ACKNOWLEDGMENTS

Project Designers

Jack Adcock—Hanging-Garden Planter Basket, pages 18–19

Dave Ashe—"Just for Her" Necklace, page 63

Dave Blell—Acorn Treasure Box, pages 9–11

Jim Boelling—Executive Nameplate, pages 50–51; Well-Ordered Cutlery Case, 84–85; Sunburst Sink Board, pages 90–93

Rob Bolson—Weed Pots Scrapwood Special, page 8

Alan Bradstreet—Whale Stamp Box, pages 52–53

Clead Christiansen—Executive Paperweight, pages 34–35

Sam Criswell—The Mini-Safe and Bill Box or Key Keeper, pages 31–33

James R. Downing—Band-Sawn Scallop Boxes, pages 5–7; Heirloom Quilt Hanger, pages 20–23; Quality-Crafted Pendulum Cradle, pages 69–73; Rolling-Pin Recipe-Card Holder, page 75; Make 'Em in a Dash Shakers, pages 76–77; Spiced-Up Napkin Holder, pages 78–79; Walnut-Clad Pump Dispenser, pages 88–89; Hot-Stuff Oak Server, pages 94–95

Kim Downing—Write Stuff Hardwood Pens, pages 54–55

Walt Easley—Get a Handle on These Sharp Steak Knives, pages 82–83

Ennis Mountain Woods—Walnut-Clad Pump Dispenser, pages 88–89

Paul Franzmeier—Sweetheart Stickpin, page 66

Marie Fredrickson—Country-Style Swan Necklace, page 64; Autumn Delight Wooden Necklace, page 65

Myles Gilmer—Perfume Decanter, pages 61–62

John Hagensick—Gardening with a Gouge, pages 14–17

Desiree Hajny—Wily-Fox Weather Vane, pages 12–13

Jim Harrold—Book of Memories, pages 24–27

Russ Hurt—Straight 'N' Narrow Noodle Cutter, pages 86–87

Bonnie Klein—Designer Earrings, page 67

Michael Mikutowski—Taking Care of Business Card Case, pages 36–37

Frank Nichols—Laminated Letter Opener, pages 29–30

Ab Odnoken—Bring on the Bracelets, page 68

Russ Peery—New Horizon Desk Set, pages 40–43

Schlabaugh and Sons—Fortune-Four Desk Accessories, pages 44–49

Roberta Zahradka—Quilt-Look Hand Mirror 59–60

Photographers

Bob Calmer
Frank Cozza
John Hetherington
Hopkins Associates
William Hopkins
Jim Kascoutas

Illustrators

Ron Chamberlain
Jamie Downing
Kim Downing
Mike Henry
Lippisch Design Inc.
Ode Designs
Carson Ode
Greg Roberts
Jim Stevenson
Yosh Sugiyama
Bill Zaun

If you would like to order any additional copies of our books, call 1-800-678-2802 or check with your local bookstore.